CONTENTS

CW00482491

Conclusion

INTRODUCTION

'A man's values are like his kidneys,' Robin Huws Jones, then principal of the National Institute for Social Work, said in his Neely Memorial lecture in 1968. 'He rarely knows he has any until they are upset.' Thomas à Kempis remarked, 'I would rather feel compunction than understand it.' Yet we must understand it, try to know what it means when we say, 'I care for another person', and struggle with all the questions which arise from such a statement.

Social work has not done over well in meeting this challenge. At least part of this reluctance might be attributed to what Eric Sainsbury, talking of the limiting definitions of values, ascribed to 'the trouble with theories', which, he wrote, may appear 'to prescribe and define practice rather than to illuminate or explain it'.[1]

I hope this book offers at least some illumination to help us consider our values, even though we know that that will not prevent them from being upset. The underlying assumption is that Christian approaches to social work and their supporting values are much neglected in discussion and that, by opening up this discussion, we may discover both something of social work values and of altruistic motivation in general.

The influence of the Judaeo-Christian tradition upon Western morality has been both seminal and pervasive and the contribution which the church and individual Christians have made to social work has been enormous. However, in more recent times references to the tradition have become less frequent in the literature of social work. From the mid-60s it is mentioned rarely, if at all. This is related to the gathering secularization of society which started earlier this century. Western thinking now tends to regard morality as situational and, at times, seems to exhibit a wariness about making any kind of moral statement. Philosophically, morality has been very definitely separated from any particular religious outlooks. Today a reading of social work literature does not give much suggestion that Christianity is a main constituent of modern social work thought. So much so, in fact, that Noel Timms' *Values in Social Work: An Enquiry*[2] omits to discuss it altogether.

In the final chapter I have attempted to look at what we mean by Christian understanding, both in the world at large and in social work in particular, and at the points of divergence and confluence between the values of Christianity and of other standpoints. These intentions, it is to be hoped, underlie the book as a whole. How we care for others, as individuals and as a society, is a matter for consideration far beyond the confines of social work. Many of the questions posed by the writers here might equally be asked of Christians who are not social workers and, because Christianity offers a challenge to all people, of those who would not call themselves Christians. For this reason, the book is not only for social workers and others whose professional lives are concerned with the welfare of others – the doctor, the nurse, the policeman, the chaplain – but also for the concerned general reader.

This book, however, does not pretend to be comprehensive. Matters which are not discussed here have been omitted more through the demands of space than for any other reason. There are at least three quite important omissions. The first is that of any discussion concerning the question of being paid to care. Alistair V. Campbell has analyzed this question in *Paid to Care?*[3]. He has considered the question specifically in relation to pastoral counselling and what the church does – or does not do – for its own members. Despite this apparently narrow focus there are many useful questions of direct relevance to social work and, as a reflection of current thinking, Mr Campbell's work is a useful starting-point.

Second, we are not involved in a one-way discussion. An assertion of the contribution of Christianity entails the humility to consider what influence social work and the social sciences and the facts of modern life – family, marriage, divorce, sexual morality – have had on the Christian view. That might well be the subject of another book.

Third, in these days of 'patch' social work, decentralized services, neighbourhood networks, and volunteer or community involvement, a chapter on the links between social workers and local churches could find a place.

Let me say something of the book's structure. The first part is an attempt to set the context by looking at the historical contribution of Christianity to social work, and to offer a comparison between the Christian view of humanity and those views expressed in other ideologies which form part of the philosophical luggage of many social workers. Other chapters consider how Christianity regards social institutions, the political imperative, and how Christianity can relate to the insights of psychoanalysis.

The second part offers examples of the place of Christianity within three areas of social work endeavour – the community, residential care and field work.

Lastly, it would be easier to list all those areas of practice –

mental illness, work with ethnic minorities, and so on – which are *not* included in the third part. This section could never intend to look comprehensively at all the areas where ethical dilemmas arise. The choice has been somewhat arbitrary but some prominent areas of practice are covered. In writing these chapters, the authors must necessarily touch upon wider issues: Peter Gilbert, for example, looking at taking children into care, had therefore to consider Christian attitudes toward the family.

In editing this book I have been all too conscious of the difficulties which lay in my path – and those of the contributors. We have intended to reassert the central place of Christian thought in social work philosophy. This is not, however, to make a special claim to exclusivity, nor to offer an exhaustive theology of social work. The answers Christianity seems to give are not uncontroversial and are open to discussion. Indeed, any reader expecting to find a philosophical or theological consensus, or all the answers to the severe dilemmas that are the everyday lot of a social worker's practice, will be disappointed. We are not intending to offer blueprints but rather reflections upon issues.

The supreme consideration for all contributors has been to discuss how Christians can respond in a practical way to what it means to be a Christian in social work today. Contributors come from a variety of different Christian traditions and the views expressed are those of the authors, not necessarily those of the editor or publisher. But all the contributors share a central affirmation about Jesus Christ. 'Who do *you* say I am?' Jesus asked the disciple Peter, who was telling him how others described him. There was a sure reply. 'The Son of the Living God.' This central affirmation we all share.

Christianity's unique contribution to man's religious development has been the doctrine of the incarnation – God taking on human form in the person of Jesus Christ. It is this which, properly understood, has caused a coming together of the divine and the human. For the pagan and the primal religions the divine was often separate and frequently fearsome, manifested in various divinities and expressed in different ways. Even for Judaism, that most worldly of faiths, God's name was not to be spoken and Abraham was allowed to see God only from behind, as he passed. The incarnation meant that men and women were not only (great though that was) to be 'reconciled to God in Christ' through believing in him, but 'the Word was actually made flesh and dwelt among us'. This is why Christians are intimately involved in the world, for not only is it a world created by God but it is also one which he felt worth saving, a salvation worked out through each of us as Christ lives in us.

Christianity has offered a world-view which gives reason for our existence and purpose but it does not seek to impose a set of solutions, to draw boundaries about all that we can be and do. Within its world-view, Christianity leaves the door fully open to the examination of conflicts, the challenge of new ideas and the creative tension that may be encountered upon the sure foundation of faith. Since social work is so often concerned with both/and answers rather than either/or questions, the values and philosophy of Christianity have as much place there as any other view.

For all of these reasons. I hope that this book will be welcomed not only by Christians who are social workers but also by those of other faiths and none.

I should like to mention especially the help I have received from Chris Hanvey who, in his helpful comments and discussion, has offered much more than his own chapter.

Terry Philpot

Notes
1   Eric Sainsbury, *Social Work Today*, 28 June 1977.
2   Noel Timms, *Values in Social Work: An Enquiry*, Routledge and Kegan Paul, 1983.
3   Alistair V. Campbell, *Paid to Care?*, SPCK, 1985.

PART 1

The Context
of Social Work

CHAPTER 1

Roots: Historical Perspective

Brian Munday

An historical review of the contribution of Christians to social work is not merely a necessary ritual at the outset of a wide-ranging book such as this. As one leading social work academic, N. Timms, commented:

> 'Questions about the "origins" of modern social work raise genuinely historical questions, but they are also important for the person considering the possibility of social work as a career. Such a person is often trying to discover how far social work can be seen as connected in some special way with Christianity or with some other general way of looking at and behaving towards the world.'[1]

It is my experience from interviewing many applicants for social work training over the years that social work today, as has been true from the beginning, continues to attract significant numbers of Christians of all ages who come with a real sense of Christian vocation. A sense of the history and origins of their chosen career can be informative as well as helping to strengthen their commitment to a profession that has come under increasing attack. This chapter takes an historical look at the involvement of Christians individually and collectively in social work, mainly in Britain, selecting themes and subjects from nineteenth and twentieth-century history which have relevance to current and immediate future interests of Christians in social work.[2]

THE LESSONS OF HISTORY

It is important that the work of Christian pioneers in social welfare in the last century should not be forgotten, even though there were serious limitations in the excessively individualistic approach to needs and problems taken by many of our Victorian predecessors.

Timms rightly urges caution in any attempt to make direct links between social work in the 1980s and older traditions. But two undoubted achievements of Christians in the last century are that they provided social work services for groups of citizens when no other services existed (for example, for poor children without families); and they pioneered important social work services for which the state gradually assumed full responsibility (for example, the probation service). These contributions will be examined more closely later.

Emphases in the development of social work

It may help here to outline briefly the different periods, phases or emphases in social work from the 1900s onwards. In doing so I draw substantially on the views of R. Jordan, whose writings on social work are recommended for their clarity and blend of experience with scholarship.[3] He refers to the great emphasis on the importance of *personal relationships* in much Victorian social work, essentially that of the Christians. This phase in social work was bound up with the development of a leisured class in Victorian Britain, especially of the educated middle-class woman. Personal relationships were central to the process of social rehabilitation, with leading Christian women offering 'perfect friendship' to the most socially and morally degraded members of society – for example, Elizabeth Fry with prisoners, Octavia Hill with slum tenants. These early social workers were often seen by their clients as exceptionally human, humble and non-patronising, on the one hand they emphasized the universality of sin; on the other they held out the hope of God's forgiveness and spiritual regeneration. And through their own empathy and kindness, they conveyed God's acceptance.

Deficiencies of this approach will be considered later, but this emphasis on personal relationships has continued strongly in social work, with references much later to the 'helping relationship' or the 'casework relationship' which has been seen as the key ingredient in much successful social work right up to the present time. But within the early emphasis on personal relationships social workers made categorical and absolute judgements on standards of behaviour, without moral or social relativity. Problems such as poverty were more likely to be seen as personal failures than as products of the economic system. A different emphasis in social work began to emerge towards the end of the nineteenth century as insights from the work of Freud and Marx cast doubts on the political and personal integrity of the privileged Victorian social worker.

Jordan refers to this next major emphasis in social work as that of *wise counselling*. The new notion of 'perfect friendship' was that of the counsellor who, armed with new understandings from the social sciences and gifted with perfect insight, '... understood the unconscious motives behind presenting symptoms, knew how to recognize transference and counter transference, could avoid over involvement and eschew subjectivity'. This transition in social work began around the end of the first world war as the numbers of social workers in state agencies increased, with a decline among those in voluntary agencies. The next chapter in this book considers Marxist and Freudian views of man and behaviour and the dilemmas these have sometimes posed for Christians in social work in this century.

In twentieth-century Britain the state has progressively taken over responsibility for social services and social work, culminating in the setting up of the Welfare State in 1948, following the Beveridge Report. This has been extended by more recent social legislation (for example, the 1970 Chronically Sick and Disabled Persons Act) which has increased state responsibility – and that of the social services departments in particular – to major client groups. The implications for changes in social work have been considerable. The great majority of social workers in Britain are now employed directly by the state, either in the social services departments or the probation service.

In the earlier post-second world war period social workers were viewed very positively as the new *social servants*, a newly-emerging profession that would make a major contribution to implementing the ideals of the Welfare State. But Jordan regards the purpose of state intervention in social welfare as having shifted since the mid-1970s. Now it is progressively more concerned with monitoring family life and 'stepping in to protect vulnerable individuals from cruel or neglectful families'. In a variety of aspects of social work in both social services departments and the probation service, the social worker is seen much more as one who checks on, monitors and controls behaviour – a shift in their role that is understandably not always appreciated by their clients. In the Barclay Report there is a reference to how

> '... vulnerable groups of people (for instance, single parents) have come increasingly to regard social workers with fear and suspicion, believing that they now have excessive powers which they may use in an arbitrary and unpredictable fashion.
> *Gingerbread, for example, told us that they warn single parents to avoid all contact with social workers.*'[4]

Of course, this is by no means the whole picture of present-day social work in Britain, but changes in the role do pose dilemmas for many social workers – including Christians – who see themselves as on the side of often very underprivileged clients of the social services in a time of widespread unemployment and related social problems. As we shall see in the following section, nineteenth-century Christian social workers have been criticized for their excessively individualistic approach to their clients' problems when an attack on social and economic conditions was really required. One of the most contentious aspects of social work since the late 1960s has been the development of a more political, radical role as social workers have sought ways of striking at the social, economic and political roots of their clients' problems.[5]

Christian pioneers in social work

The Wolfenden Report on voluntary organizations[6] named four contributions that such organizations can make to social welfare provision:

1. As a pressure group, pressing for changes in policy and provisions.

2. As a pioneer of new services, often with the intention that they should eventually be taken on by statutory agencies.

3. As the provider of services complementary, additional or alternative to statutory services.

4. As the sole provider of services.

Historically Christians and Christian organizations (including, of course, churches) in the broad field of social work have acted in all four ways. In the nineteenth century their emphasis was on the sole provision of services and on pioneering, whereas in more recent times Christian voluntary organizations have concentrated on providing complementary or additional social and social work services to those of the state.

Heasman's book[7] is a rich source of material on Christian (mainly evangelical) involvement in social work in nineteenth-century Britain. Only a flavour of that contribution can be conveyed here, including some of the criticisms of the social work of an earlier period. Heasman observes that it was as Christians began to feel that problems such as poverty and poor housing were not in keeping with the teaching of the churches, that social work became more closely associated with Christian belief in the second half of the last century.

At different points in the century Christians such as Octavia Hill, Mary Carpenter, Canon Barnett and the Booths recognized the needs of a wide variety of very deprived groups of citizens, and so began to organize a response to these glaring needs and problems. Sometimes new voluntary organizations were started, often related to outstanding contributions by individual pioneers and reformers (for example, Lord Shaftesbury); or existing churches and missions moved progressively into social work as part of their local ministry. It is interesting to note that in the second half of the nineteenth century revivalists such as D.L. Moody encouraged converts to engage in some form of social work, particularly among young people. Heasman estimates that as many as three quarters of voluntary charitable organizations in that period were run by evangelical Christians, many formed after the revival in mid-century.

A list of the main groups of people for whom nineteenth-century evangelical Christians provided social work services reads like the chapter headings of a modern text on the responsibilities of the statutory social services: deprived children, teenagers, prostitutes, prisoners, elderly people, physically and mentally ill, and blind and deaf people – and very many more. In every case there was little or no provision by the state for these groups, at best the Poor Law service. In Wolfenden report terms Christians were the sole providers of services, in some cases pioneering a desperately neeeded provision that later would be taken on by the state. Meanwhile, in *laissez-faire* Victorian Britain, anything other than safety-net, minimal state intervention was seen as an unwise intrusion into some kind of natural order that should not be tampered with.

Much of this social work was carried out by Christian women, mainly from privileged and protected backgrounds, with little training other than that of managing a large Victorian household. Their emphasis on offering 'perfect friendship' has been referred to earlier, with that essentially human touch which had been lacking in much earlier voluntary charity. It is interesting that social workers today work within what are termed 'the *personal* social services', the reference to 'personal' differentiating these services from those such as housing and income maintenance where there is much less individualising of service.

If these privileged women performed most of the 'casework', individual churches and missions initiated all kinds of services for specific groups or for the needy population in their area. It was Canon Barnett, vicar of Whitechapel in East London, who founded the first settlement of Toynbee Hall and started the settlement movement which has had an important influence on social work and community work in Britain and other countries. Several of the missions started specialist forms of social work – for example, Dr Barnardo's work with deprived children, which was an offshoot of his East End Juvenile Mission. The London City Mission – which still engages in a mix of evangelism and Christian social work – started in 1835 and spread to many other cities where they became the central organization for social work. From the East London Christian Mission, William and Catherine Booth started the Salvation Army in 1865, a Christian organization still providing services today which complement those of statutory agencies and, arguably, make basic provision for the homeless and destitute in some areas where nothing else exists.

But not all Christians were happy with the standard approach to social work of the missions, churches and the women workers. In understanding the contribution of nineteeth-century Christians to the development of social work we should recognize that there were groups such as the Christian Socialists, with the Rev. F.D. Maurice and others showing that there was much in common between Christian theology and socialist ideals. Heasman refers to *The Bitter Cry of Outcast London*, a penny pamphlet of 1883 (probably written by a Congregational minister) which opened as follows:

'Whilst we have been building our churches and solacing ourselves with our religion and dreaming that the millennium was coming, the poor have been growing poorer, and the wretched more miserable, and the immoral more corrupt.'

The words of Wesleyan John Scott Lidgett, also quoted by Heasman, have probably been echoed by countless social workers of all beliefs right up to the present day:

'I am not willing that it [social work] should be merely an ambulance to gather up the casualties of our industrial system, without being equally anxious to lessen the causes of these casualties.'

In various ways the so-called progressive, more socialist, evangelical Christians tried to overcome the individualism of the

Christian voluntary organizations and concentrate the attack on the roots of poverty and deprivation, to include greater state intervention and provision as required. The roots of individuals' problems were seen in flawed, very imperfect social and economic structures of society as well as in the tendency for humankind to create its own personal problems through sin.

From police court missionary to probation officer

The history of the English probation service is a good illustration of Christians pioneering a social work service that was eventually taken over and extended by the state. As Joan King records,[8] probation supervision originated in nineteenth-century experimentation in both legal and religious fields, seeking a constructive alternative to the harsh penalties of the criminal code. The first legal experiment was in 1820, to be followed much later in 1876 when the Church of England Temperance Society appointed the first police court missionary to visit some of the London police courts to attempt reclamation of drunkards. From then on there was a steady expansion of this Christian service, beyond the original idea of dealing only with drink problems. By 1900 there were 100 men and nineteen women working as police court missionaries, in addition to a smaller number sponsored by other religious bodies.

By now there was a change in attitude towards the responsibility of the state for social welfare, including the reformation of offenders. The work of the police court missionaries had demonstrated the practical possibilities of supervision in the open, leading to the easy acceptance by Parliament in 1907 of a statutory probation system in Britain. The Children's Act of the following year provided for probation officers in the London juvenile courts to be paid out of public funds for the first time. The 1907 Act formed the basis not only of the British probation service but for services in other parts of the world. As King observed:

'The contents and scope of the Probation and Offenders Act 1907 were a testimony to the thoroughness with which the pioneers of probation had done their work.'

The contribution of nineteenth-century Christians to social work

References have already been made to criticisms of the essentially individualistic approach of the nineteenth-century Christians, criticisms made by other contemporary Christians as well as by present-day writers. Jordan, for example, observes that it never seemed to occur to the Victorian pioneers of social work that collective state provision to alleviate social problems like poverty might be more effective than their sterling individual efforts. This seeming myopia stemmed from a limited form of Christian belief, wedded to a view of society as an organic whole whose natural processes would be upset by compulsory collective action. Lubove[9] is also very critical of the heavy emphasis on the personal relationship and friendship in so much nineteenth-century social work, both in Britain and America. His book is mainly about the history of American social work, important in Britain because of British reliance upon American experience and publications in the earlier post-war period.

Heasman acknowledges the validity of these criticisms, recognizing the failure of evangelical Christians to follow up their widespread social work with a definite social policy; and their ready acceptance of the prevailing class structure. This changed with the growth of the 'forward movement' of the churches in the 1880s which applied salvation to society as well as to individuals. If evangelical Christians were sometimes also guilty of usurping the duties of the state it was because of the glaring inadequacies in the Poor Law system.

More positively Heasman and others refer to the most striking feature of evangelical charity – its vast dimensions, with hardly a need which was not catered for in some way. They played an important part in drawing public attention to social problems and helped to create a climate of public opinion that led to a gradual acceptance of state responsibility for social welfare and social work. They first recognized social work as a distinctive professional occupation, offering training and payment to workers. Christian social workers today can gain much encouragement and inspiration from the social work of their nineteenth-century predecessors.

INTEGRATION OR SEPARATION?

Individual Christians and Christian voluntary organizations have long been concerned as to whether they can best make a distinctive contribution to social work and social welfare by working within or in very close partnership with the state system; or whether they should set up and work in separate Christian agencies that are outside and not dependent upon the state. This has also been a major concern of other groups with quite different beliefs, for example, Marxists in social work in the politically more radical 1970s. This dilemma about integration or separation arises because individual social workers with strong beliefs feel that the practice implications of these beliefs cannot always be expressed when they are working within a secular profession, usually in large, bureaucratic, politically controlled social service organizations.

Keith White, writing about residential care for children, is concerned about how

> 'Working conditions, career grades, unionisation, funding and
> bureaucracy have combined to institutionalise the caring
> process in such a way that we wonder whether we are helping
> or harming many children.'[10]

He argues that voluntary organizations should be as free as possible from local authority funding and the local authority mould. He also advocates that Christian voluntary organizations such as Dr Barnardo's and the Church of England Children's Society should re-establish their spiritual links at all levels, integrating Christian traditions, faith and practice. Such organizations are certainly less explicitly Christian than formerly.

Alan Storkey[11] comes out strongly for the setting up of 'Christian alternatives' in many fields of life, including social welfare. He refers to the need for Christian newspapers, a trade union and political party, because without the development of a wide range of Christian alternatives large numbers of Christians will continue to live essentially secular and humanist lives for most of the week, lives that remain compromised by non-Christian practices and policies. Most Christians in social work recognize the strength of Storkey's warnings but believe that God calls them to maintain a Christian presence in state agencies, however difficult this may be.

For some years now it has been the policy of Conservative and Labour governments in Britain to encourage the growth of the contribution of the voluntary sector to social welfare. This has been particularly marked under recent Conservative governments. There are both dangers and opportunities for Christians and their voluntary organizations in this policy. The great danger is that, for both political and economic reasons, Government is reducing its commitment to state-funded social welfare and it is to the detriment of the most disadvantaged groups in society. This is a trend that should be firmly resisted. The opportunities for the voluntary sector are the possibility of church-state partnerships springing up, similar to the experiment in Tonbridge, Kent.

In 1978 the local Baptist church and the social services office agreed to enter into an experiment to see whether a social worker attached to the church (on a new housing estate) would be able to build up a community care network for people living on the estate. The social worker was a member of the church but employed by the social services department, with the church paying forty per cent of the salary. The overall aim of the project was to enable the social services department and the church to work together for the benefit of the community. One obvious advantage was that the social worker was able to mobilize voluntary resources from within the church – for example, accommodation was provided for a teenage boy who otherwise would have been taken into care. This approach could usefully be adopted elsewhere with statutory agencies and their social workers forming close working relations with Christian ministers. The social worker in such an arrangement may not necessarily be a committed Christian, but at least a sympathy towards Christianity and the local church is required.

In future there are likely to be more opportunities for Christian social workers to work in the voluntary sector because of its overall growth, and because there may well be the development of more Christian 'alternatives' in social welfare. For example, a Christian Council on Ageing was formed in 1983[12] in recognition that old people need help with their intangible and specifically spiritual needs which the statutory services are frequently not able to meet. This may be more of a complementary than an alternative Christian service but the distinction is often imprecise. But for the present most Christians whose vocation is to work in social work do so either in the state, secular social services departments or the probation service.

Vocation, 'burn-out' and the Christian's resources for social work

One of the recurring questions about social work has been the extent to which it is essentially a vocation, a profession or simply a fairly ordinary occupation that has become increasingly trade-unionised and mostly located in large local authority departments. This has been an issue of particular concern to Christians, highlighted by crises of conscience in recent years over strikes by social workers and the inevitable hardships caused for their clients. (See Chapter 12 for a discussion of this issue.)

No doubt the nineteenth-century Christian social workers saw their work very much as a true vocation, emphasising such characteristics as a sense of personal fitness and a God-given obligation to engage in work that could be very stressful – sometimes even a danger to one's health – and offering little by way of tangible rewards. The sense of making a personal sacrifice in entering social work might also be involved. This view of social work as primarily a vocation has continued strongly in this century, until about the last fifteen to twenty years. (When I was training for work in the probation service in the early 1960s, I well recall an older Christian probation officer refusing a 12½% pay award on the grounds that 'it would attract the wrong kind of people into the service'.) Historically, Christians have often seen occupations such as nursing, teaching and social work, jobs where personal qualities are still seen as of very great importance, as ones in which they have something special to offer. Whereas in the past applicants for nursing and probation officer posts may sometimes have been closely questioned because they were not Christians and therefore were not seen to have the requisite qualities, there are applicants for social work training today whose sense of Christian vocation may come under the most careful scrutiny. This is an interesting shift in the perception of the role of the social worker.

Unfortunately a person's sense of vocation can and has been exploited when it comes to rates of pay and working conditions, one reason why social work is now referred to more as a profession or a unionised occupation. Nokes has put his finger on the problem:

> 'The danger of the humanitarian tradition, the danger in the idea of vocation is that the human element becomes the area in which the slack is regularly taken up'.[13]

The history of residential care in social work graphically illustrates Nokes' point. However, non-Christian and Christian commentators on social work recognize the importance of the personal qualities needed by those who want to become social workers. Jordan, for example, refers to an awesome list of qualities he looks for in applicants for social work training, including an ability to learn from one's mistakes; a capacity for honest self-doubt and self-criticism; a passionate concern about some aspects of the suffering and injustice in society; and a resilience in face of failure.

Apart from weighing up whether candidates I interview for social work possess these kinds of qualities, I also consider what personal resources applicants have that will enable them to remain committed and helpful to their clients. There has been a good deal of discussion about the incidence of something called 'burn-out' in social work which Zastrow explains in this way:

> 'Burn-out involves the loss of concern for the people with whom one is working. In addition to physical exhaustion (and sometimes illness), burn-out is characterised by an emotional exhaustion in which the professional no longer has any positive feelings, sympathy or respect for clients or patients'.[14]

In social work this kind of experience results not just from the impact on the social worker of working intensively with stressful problems but also from frustrating working conditions and constantly not having access to adequate resources to meet clients' needs.

Although Christians as well as non-Christians in social work experience 'burn-out' at times, historically the committed Christian has been able to draw on the wealth of spiritual resources available to him or her to keep alive their love for their clients and their enthusiasm for the job. This is quite clear from accounts of the lives of the earlier Christian social workers and more recently, for example, from personal accounts by members of the Social Workers' Christian Fellowship. Being able to draw on these spiritual resources is vital for the Christian in social work if he or she is not only to cope positively with the job on a day-to-day basis but go even further and show that 'bias to the poor' and readiness to work in the most deprived areas of Britain that has been so powerfully advocated by David Sheppard, the Bishop of Liverpool. Christians who do that will be identifying with the best aspects of the social work pioneered by their nineteenth-century forefathers.

Notes

[1] N. Timms, *Social Work*, Routledge and Kegan Paul, London 1970.
[2] A short historical view of this kind is inevitably very incomplete. Readers requiring more detailed knowledge should consult such books as K. Heasman, *Evangelicals in Action*, Geoffrey Bles, London, 1962.
[3] B Jordan, *Invitation to Social Work*, Martin Robertson, Oxford 1984.
[4] Barclay Committee, *Social Workers – Their Role and Tasks*, Bedford Square Press London, 1982, pp. 188-189 (author's italics).
[5] See B. Jordan and N. Parton, *The Political Dimensions of Social Work*, Basil Blackwell, Oxford, 1983.
[6] Wolfenden Committee, *The Future of Voluntary Organisations*, Groom Helm, London, 1977.

[7] See above.

[8] J. King (ed.), *The Probation Service*, Butterworth, London 1958.

[9] R. Lubove, *The Professional Altruist*, Harvard University Press, Cambridge, USA, 1965.

[10] K. White, 'Looking for Somewhere To Be', *Community Care*, 27 October 1983.

[11] A. Storkey, *A Christian Social Perspective*, Inter-Varsity Press, 1979.

[12] See D. Bell, 'A Sign of Hope', *Community Care*, 28 April 1983.

[13] P. Nokes, *The Professional Task in Welfare Practice*, Routledge and Kegan Paul, London, 1967.

[14] C. Zastrow, 'Understanding and Preventing Burn-Out', *British Journal of Social Work*, No. 14, 1985, pp. 141-155.

CHAPTER 2

The Untenable Dilemma

W.J.Patterson

In 1958 a sub-committee of the Commission on Social Work Practice of the National Association of Social Workers in the USA sought to come to an operational definition of social work. The Commission chairman, H.M. Barlett, reduced the elements in the basis of social work practice to two. Commenting in her book, *The Common Base of Social Work Practice*, on the Commission's findings and conclusions she wrote:

> 'The Committee recognized that mature professions rest on strong bodies of knowledge and values from which scientific and ethical principles that guide the operation of the practitioner are derived. In this sense knowledge and values take priority over method and are the major definers of method and technique.'[1]

Social work then rests on a dual foundation of knowledge and values. Knowledge is a body of scientific fact and theory open to empirical testing, demonstration and replication. Professional values delineate the principles on which professional behaviour should be based. For social work practice relevant and necessary fact-and-theory has been incorporated from the social sciences and it can be said that social work is, to an extent, applied social science. The fact that social work's body of knowledge is largely (and increasingly) a scientific body of fact-and-theory about humankind and society is extremely important, as will become clear in what follows. Values are defined as those principles of action and attitude which the agency expects or requires of its social workers in their dealings with clients.

These two components of social work theory and practice, are mutually at odds. I believe that each makes a statement about the nature of man (and by 'man', of course, I mean people, irrespective of gender) and that these two concepts conflict, since they flow from two essentially different world-views.

I believe that it is impossible to practise social work consistently on the basis of both views and that the practitioner must continually shift from one view to the other. The two views of the nature of man are here called social work's 'Ethical Man' and

'Scientific Man'. Several variations of this dichotomy are implicit and explicit in the literatures of psychology, social work and casework, a number of which are examined and analyzed before an alternative approach to the problem and a solution within a biblical Christian world-view is proposed.

'ETHICAL MAN'

A cluster of concepts appears regularly in social work literature in terms of which the client is conceived. These concepts include 'respect for persons'; 'client self-direction' or 'self-determination'; 'individualization'; 'human dignity'; 'the rights of individuals'; 'acceptance' and 'confidentiality'.

It would seem, as the Code of Ethics for Irish Social Workers states, that when 'the social worker undertakes to respect the dignity and worth of the human person', he is committing himself to the central value of social work and is affirming a certain belief in the nature of humanity. This belief is reinforced by the fact that the client is to be accorded the right to decide, to be accepted for who he is irrespective of his actions or attitudes, and that his confidences are to be taken seriously and protected.

This is a high view of human nature – as an entity with the capacity to determine the course of his life (within limitations) and possessing an intrinsic value simply through being himself apart from his roles and actions. From this view there is a compulsion to reach out even to those whose actions are extremely anti-social (whether as offenders or as psychiatrically disturbed); or to those who are dependent and by most criteria unproductive (whether the severely handicapped, children or the elderly). According to social work values the intrinsic dignity and worth of the individuals in these groupings is untouched by the fact that they fall into these or any other groupings. A person has being apart from his roles and actions, and hence has dignity and worth apart from his behaviour. McLeod and Meyer summarize this in their study of the values of social workers:

'A primary value mentioned centrally in any discussion of social work values is belief in the worth and dignity of the individual human being, without regard for differentiating criteria'.[2]

'SCIENTIFIC MAN'

This model appears in guises as diverse as behaviourism, psychoanalysis and Marxism, notwithstanding their mutual disagreements on many points. What, however, is crucial is the common theme in regard to their views of the basic nature of the human individual. Behaviourism and psychoanalysis are both schools of psychology and as such have had their major impact on social work in the area of casework with families and individuals. Marxism is a political philosophy and so focuses more on the relation of people to society and its institutions. In variously diluted forms this has touched primarily the areas of social work such as welfare rights, and patch- and community-based interventions. B.F. Skinner and Sigmund Freud will be considered as representatives of the two psychological schools. The model of man in Marxism will be approached somewhat differently. As Hollis says: 'The first question to be raised about these scientific principles is often the philosophical one of whether the assumption of lawfulness in behaviour and of cause and effect relationships in behaviour does not mean that casework has become completely deterministic?'[3]

Behaviourism

Skinner, from the outset, attacks the idea of 'autonomous man'. He denies the existence of man apart from conditioned responses to his environment—in other words, he attacks a concept of man as existing apart from his roles and actions. He therefore attacks that view of man which has been shown to pervade the ethics of social work. Some selections from his writings bring this home with force.

> 'Two features of autonomous man are particularly troublesome. In the traditional view, a person is free. He is autonomous in the sense that his behaviour is uncaused. He can, therefore, be held responsible for what he does ... By questioning the control exercised by autonomous man and demonstrating the control exercised by the environment, a science of behaviour also seems to question dignity or worth.'[4]

Skinner is consistent with his presuppositions. He, of course, admits that social scientists have not uncovered all of the many and continual environmental controls which mould man's behaviour; he even acknowledges that 'many anthropologists, sociologists and psychologists have used their expert knowledge to prove that man is free, purposeful and responsible', yet he calls this an 'escape route' which 'is slowly closed as new evidences of the predictability of human behaviour are discovered. Personal exemption from a complete determinism is revoked as a scientific analysis progresses, particularly in accounting for the behaviour of the individual'.[5]

Not all behaviourist psychologists would go as far as Skinner. Margaret Yelloly, for example, argues that the 'analysis of any relationship in scientific terms alone must remain unsatisfactory and partial as a guide to action. Our conception of what is desirable in relationship between persons cannot depend solely on answers to such questions as, What is effective? or What is therapeutic? but on the value that is placed on human personality, and on our conception of the nature of man and of interpersonal encounters. This has to do with values and the ethical basis of action and goes far beyond the scope of scientific analysis.'[6]

Skinner, however, would point out that such half-way houses are not logical on behaviouristic premises; all behaviour is constituted of responses to the environment and all talk of morality or ethical bases of action is no less illusionary than talk of 'the mind', of 'an idea', or 'fear' (ie, emotions).[7] All these Skinner recasts in terms of behaviour. Each man is a unique bundle of behaviours determined by environment; only that and nothing more.

Psychoanalysis

Psychoanalysis would fundamentally disagree with this emphasis on environmental determinism, and would point to other mainly internal forces moulding behaviour. Some, such as the neo-Freudians, would give more weight to environmental influences, but Martin Shaw, in the symposium mentioned above, himself committed to a behavioural approach in social work, argues that, with regard to their basic view of man, behaviourism and psychoanalysis say the same thing:

'The social worker, adopting a behavioural approach, wedded inevitably to a determinist view, is criticized above all for apparently regarding people as machines to be programmed, manipulated and controlled at the will of the controller.

'It is tempting in this context, though perhaps insufficient, to defend the determinist view by pointing out that traditional casework theory and practice is equally determinist, to the extent that it is founded on psychoanalytic theory. Freud would certainly have been sympathetic to the comment made by

Skinner (1956), a leading exponent of behaviour control, that caprice is only another name for behaviour for which we have not yet found a cause.'[8]

Sandler, Dare and Holder pick up the same thread and make it more explicit. Freud, they show, took the idea of determinism from the physical sciences and applied it to psychology:

> 'The assumption of psychological determinism is still a cornerstone of psychoanalytic thinking. Briefly it is the belief that every aspect of behaviour or subjective experience, and every aspect of the functioning of the mental apparatus, can be seen as the outcome of the events (psychological as well as non-psychological) which precede it.'[9]

This raises a problem, for it is a sociological fact that most individuals believe that they have and exercise their capacity of free decision. Whether or not this is objectively true, it is a fact that most people believe they have freedom of choice, at least in some areas. How does the psychoanalyst view this? As Halmos observes in *The Faith of the Counsellors:*

> 'Because of the assumption of the existence of unconscious mental functioning ..., the psychoanalyst would take the view that many actions which appear on the surface to be a consequence of free acts of will are inevitably determined by the influence of unconscious psychological forces acting on the individual.'[10]

If self-determination is an illusion, then the 'Ethical Man' does not exist. 'Scientific Man' kills 'Ethical Man' – they cannot *logically* co-exist. One view denies self-determination and man's intrinsic dignity and worth, the other posits it – both cannot be true!

Carl Rogers puts it this way:

> 'In our pursuit of science we are fools if we do not assume everything that occurs is a portion of a cause-and-effect sequence, and that nothing occurs outside of that ... but ... if we adopt that point of view in our living as human beings, in our confrontation with life, then that is death.'[11]

Quite so, but surely it follows then that to apply such deterministic theories and their associated techniques to our clients is a form of (at least attempted) murder of their basic humanity.

Marxism

In the thought of Marx there would appear to be a distinct view of human nature. He believed that under capitalism man was alienated from his essential nature and dignity but that in the classless society of communism, man would reclaim his true humanity, *as he was fully merged into the collective* for the first time.

Marx posited that the essence of man is the sum total of all his social relations. For example in his *Selected Works* he says:

> 'In the social production of their life, men enter into definite relations that are indispensible and independent of their will, relations of production which correspond to a definite stage of development of their material productive forces. The sum total of these relations of production constitutes the economic structure of society, the real foundation, on which rises a legal and political superstructure and to which correspond definite forms of social consciousness. The mode of production of material life conditions the social, political and intellectual life process in general. *It is not the consciousness of men that determines their being, but on the contrary, their social being that determines their consciousness.*'[12]

Here is the statement that man is the sum of his social relations or roles, and that he does not have identity apart from these roles. Moreover the relations of production – that is, a person's role in the production process either as entrepreneur or worker – are the most significant in that they determine his consciousness (ideas, values and beliefs). Man's ideas are merely reflections in his mind of the economic system in which he exists and are totally dependent on it. These in turn are expressed in society in legal, political and religious institutions and beliefs. The doctrine is therefore one of economic determinism.

This view of man, which sees him only as the product of his social relations or roles (primarily his work and class roles), is irreconcilable with social work's 'Ethical Man' as described above, which insists that man 'is at least in part identifiable as a person who can stand back from his particular role identifications.'[13] So we encounter again two incompatible views. Marxism as a materialist and a deterministic theory has no logical place for the 'Ethical Man.' As A.B. Zalkind, quoted in Bales' *Communism and the Reality of Moral Law* puts it: 'For the proletariat human life does not have a metaphysical, self-sufficient value'. J.D. Bales commenting on this says: 'Even in the future Communist paradise personality is not in reality given to man, since in that future society each man is merged with every other man in the collective. Not only is bitter conflict absent from that society, but also the distinction between one man and another. The individual personality is lost in the collective.'[14]

DETERMINISM

Each of these three prominent influences on social work thought and practice—behaviourism, psychoanalysis and Marxism although they conflict at numerous points, express a view of man as being determined. This may be expounded as environmental determinism by Skinner, psychological determinism by Freud and economic determinism by Marx. We could extend outside the field of social work to the biological determinism of Darwin. There is a cost, however, in any deterministic mould of thinking or, indeed, in any amalgam and that is the loss of the humanity of man, the loss of man as having intrinsic dignity, value and worth, the loss of the 'Ethical Man' – a view to which social workers are supposedly committed.

This leads to three major questions. First, is this not just an abstract academic problem, without any real substance in the reality of day-to-day practice? Second, does a scientific approach lead inevitably to a deterministic view of man? Third, is there any adequate basis for a high view of man – Ethical Man – or is this just an irrationally held belief on the part of those who cannot or will not face reality?

Is the problem real?

It will be helpful at this stage to introduce three examples to underline my assertion that the dichotomy between the 'Scientific Man' and the 'Ethical Man' outlined above is one which arises in everyday practice and is not just a theoretical, conceptual or philosophical problem. Clare Winnicott in an essay on 'Casework and agency function' depicts just such a dichotomy arising in a probation officer/probationer relationship. It appears that she is not fully aware of the nature of the issues involved. She records:

'When a child or an adult *commits an offence* of a certain degree and kind, he brings into action the machinery of law. The probation officer who is then asked to do casework with the client feels he ought to apply techniques implying the casework principle of self-determination, but he loses everything if he forgets his relationship to his agency and the court, since *symptoms of this kind of illness* are unconsciously designed to bring authority into the picture.'[15]

Raymond Plant gives another example, using John Bowlby's interpretation of the situation of unmarried mothers:

'It is emotionally disturbed men and women who produce illegitimate children ... the girl who has an illegitimate baby often comes from an unsatisfactory home background and has developed a neurotic character, the illegitimate baby being in the nature of *a symptom of her neurosis*.'[16]

As Plant says, a great 'contrast' is to be perceived:

'What appears to be an action of an *agent committing* something is reinterpreted in terms of some kind of *illness*; that is something which happens to a person, something which he *did not do* in the full sense of the word, and for which *eo ipso* he cannot be held responsible. In so far as this involves a diminution of responsibility, it also involves a diminution of respect for persons.'[17]

This, translated into the terminology of this chapter, means that in practice a client cannot be treated as a 'Scientific man' (here, determined in a mechanistic model with medical labels) and as an 'Ethical man' (what is called a 'human being' or a 'person') at the same time.

This is essentially the same observation as made by Goffman of psychiatric patients in his book, *Asylums*:

'Although there is a psychiatric view of mental disorder... freeing the offender from moral responsibility for his offence, total institutions can little afford this particular kind of determinism. Inmates must be caused to self-direct themselves in a manageable way, and, for this to be promoted, both desired and undesired conduct must be defined as springing from the personal will and character of the individual inmate himself, and defined as something he can himself do something about.'[18]

Thus the patient is defined as sick so that he may be admitted to the hospital, and once there he is defined as responsible so that he can be encouraged to work for his release. Likewise it would seem that the social worker changes from one view of man to the other depending on his perception of the exigencies of the specific situation he is in. It would seem that the problem is real.

Science versus Pseudo-Science – Determinism or not?

'Supposing science ever became complete so that it knew every single thing in the whole universe. Is it not plain that the questions "Why is there a universe?" "Why does it go on as it does?" "Has it any meaning?" would remain just as they were?

'Now the position would be quite hopeless but for this. There is one thing, and only one, in the whole universe which we know more about than we could learn from external observation. This one thing is Man. We do not merely observe man, we *are* men. In this case we have, so to speak, inside information; we are in the know.'[19]

Here we have a check on the validity of the social sciences; we are the object as well as the subject of study. This is why there is a unique distinction between the social sciences and all the other sciences. Here, if we are honest, we are forced to recognize the existence of additional information, other facts. These facts of experience such as thinking, morals, choice and belief are just as real as the facts of external observation with which science normally deals, and a true view of man has to account for them also.

Moreover, the two classes of facts are not isolated from one another, for in normal living we act on the basis of a synthesis of internal realities and external observations. They are two sides of the same coin, two aspects of the same reality, me. Me considered by me, and me considered by another; these perspectives are true for every individual and leave us with an important consideration about science. Science applied to man opens up to us only certain aspects of the total reality of man for it is selective with regard to the classes of facts regarded as valid and does not tell us all there is to know about man. The tool of observation is not sufficient to do this. When we claim that science is the measure of man, we find in our own experience facts which are exceedingly embarrassing, and conflict with the theory. As Carl Rodgers observed above, scientific methodology applied in our daily living is death!

What can be done? Deny the facts that do not fit the theory

and so keep the theory intact? This closed-mindedness will constitute a refusal to face reality, a reactionary attitude towards personal change which is counter to a genuine 'scientific spirit'. We will call this position 'Pseudo-Science'. The only other alternative is to accept the facts and face the truth that the theory which denies them is inadequate and needs serious revision. Moreover, if there is more to man than meets the eye of science, science will have to remain open-ended. The discussion here turns on the fact of the uniqueness of any science of man.

The one case where the scientist has inside knowledge is in the study of man, and there he finds that his tools take him so far but no further. In passing, it should be noted that this should keep the scientist from making *a priori* statements or assumptions about all those other phenomena in the universe with regard to which he has no 'inside' information. Thus, the physical or natural scientist also cannot exclude the possibility that there may be significant facts and processes united with the observable phenomena but by their nature not open to scientific detection. True science acknowledges that it loses or misses or is only competent to study part of the total reality. True science brings to light that there is more to reality than what science brings to light. In the study of man, for this is highly pertinent to the social work profession, one must be aware that science at best gives only a partial picture. If the scientist or the philosopher limits reality purely to the observable realm where cause and effect appear to operate he will end up engulfing both himself and his own thought also, or else by having to live *outside* his own views of the nature of man thus negating it. Consider the following:

> 'In *The Listener*, (September 30th, 1971), he [Skinner] says
> 'We must hope that a culture will emerge in which those who
> have power will use it for the general good ... If the power of a
> technology of behaviour does indeed fall into the hands of
> despots, it will be because it has been rejected by men and
> women of good will'... Has Skinner himself found some magic
> way to be able to accept or reject beyond conditioning?
> Although he does not know it, he is here speaking as a man
> made in the image of God.'[20]

> 'Freud, not really believing in love, saying that the end
> of all things is sex, but yet needing real love, writes to his
> fiancée, "When you come to me, little Princess, love me
> *irrationally*".'[21]

'If the doctrine [of economic determinism] is true, it is false.
Marx's thoughts were determined by the economic system and
his relationship to it, if his ideas were but a reflection of the
material world, his doctrine of economic determinism was
simply one of the reflections in his mind of the economic
system. Since it was a reflection of a passing class interest, and
not an eternal truth, the doctrine of economic determinism is
simply a bourgeois prejudice. Karl Marx's thinking can
not be an exception to what is universally true concerning
thought. Therefore, it was impossible for his thinking to
transcend the class-cause of his own thought and thus he could
not have discovered a universal truth which transcended class
"truth". Not only would it be class "truth" but it would be class
"truth" of the bourgeoisie, for Marx was not of the proletariat,
but of the bourgeoisie.'[22]

Thus in these, out of many examples, Skinner and Freud are
shown not to be able to live inside their theories, and Marx by his
own theory totally undermines himself. Halmos concludes: 'It
would seem that the theoretician ... must be allowed freedom
from his theories so that he can have as much abundance of life as
anybody else.'[23] Pseudo-science produces an untenable dilemma
between determinism on the one hand and what we find ourselves
to be in living – and it is the living that exposes the doctrine. True
science is aware of its limitations especially in explaining man and
does not preclude the unseen (unobservable) or transcendant *a
priori* by its philosophical starting point, because it acknowledges
that our 'inside information' is just as real as that which is
observable.

Is there a basis for 'Ethical Man'?

If what has been argued above is accurate, then what is needed is
a philosophy or view of man and the universe which can give a
basis for the validity of true science and also for the reality of the
people we are in our daily lives. Moreover, we cannot create this
just to satisfy our need – to have confidence that it is real we
would expect such a 'philosophy' or explanation to be in a
terminology that predates that of social work. Bertrand Russell,
of all people, points us in a new direction.

'If we seek justification for believing in the sacred rights of
human beings to be respected as persons having intrinsic value,

we must seek it in the higher religions, for we cannot find it in science.'[24]

The 'science' referred to by Russell is that which I have called Pseudo-science. The Judaeo-Christian belief in the nature of the universe is that it is created – that is, it has not always existed – so it follows that impersonal matter is not the origin of all that is. Alone in the created universe man is created in the likeness of the Creator who is personal – it is that which gives him his uniqueness and dignity. The person that we find ourselves to be in living no longer stands in dissociation or discontinuity with that which has always existed, but in fact, corresponds to that which has always been there, and so has true meaning. When the Christian affirms that man is 'created in the image of God' he is affirming that man, though finite and subject to the pressures of cause and effect processes, is himself also a true first cause in the areas of choice and action. Here man does not have to stand outside his explanation of himself to be what he is.

There is however a problem – if being created in the image of God provides a basis for man being a person, including the capacity to reason, feel and self-determine, is this not also the source of the twisted, the cruel and the ugly in man? In the deterministic views referred to above and in the general contemporary view of the nature of man, it is assumed that man now is essentially the same as he has always been in spite of quantitative changes due to development, civilization, history or evolution, and that the perverse and ugly in man has always been part of it. In the biblical revelation, what man is now is different in principle from what God made him to be – and it was man who made the choice which made that difference.

This initial act of rebellion is, in the biblical Christian framework, the 'Fall' of man, not from his 'imageness' but from fellowship with his Creator. This is the source of his cruelty and selfishness. It is now man, not God, who is responsible for introducing the barbaric and the selfish. The Christian answer means that, as a social worker, I can face a client whose life is falling apart (even because of himself) and know (without any leap) that he is important because he is made in the image of God. Furthermore, there is no need to remove his dignity or responsibility by calling him 'sick' or 'deprived' or 'an inadequate personality,' as if those labels are all that he is and there is no need to blame it on God.

Schaeffer presents four propositions concerning the Christian assertion that man at a point of space-time history has changed himself and is now morally abnormal:

'First, we now can explain ... that man is cruel, without God being a bad God. Secondly, there is hope of a solution for this moral problem which is not intrinsic to the mannishness of man. If his cruelty is intrinsic to ... what man always has been ... then there is no hope of a solution. But if it is an abnormality there is hope of a solution. It is in this setting that the substitutionary, propitiatory death of Christ ceases to be ... incomprehensible.

'The third point that flows from this is that on this basis we can have a real ground for fighting evil, including social evil and social injustice. The person who sees man as normal...has no real basis for fighting evil. But the Christian has...God did not make man cruel, and He did not make the results of man's cruelty. These are abnormal, contrary to what God made, and as such we can fight the evil without fighting God.

'The fourth result is that we can have real morals and moral absolutes, for God is now absolutely good, with the total exclusion of evil from God. God's character is the moral absolute of the universe.'[25]

It is important to underline where the Christian world view leads. It provides a basis for Ethical Man – that is, man having dignity and intrinsic worth apart from anything he may have done. It establishes the distinction between true guilt and guilt feelings (or psychological guilt) and contains a solution. And it provides a basis for true open-ended science as opposed to Pseudo-science, in that study by scientific observation, classification, inference and reasoning corresponds to a universe created by a reasoning God. In other words, a unified field of knowledge is possible and there is no need for a leap of faith, for intellectual schizophrenia, in order to have a consistent view of man which also is compatible with the people we are in our daily lives.

It is true that many social workers more or less hold to one or other view of Scientific Man as well as the values of social work and the view of man implicit there, not more than vaguely aware of the intellectual dichotomy they thereby embrace.

There are those from other philosophical starting-points, notably liberal humanists and some of those looking to the East for a basis for spiritual values, who would wish to affirm a high view of man and would espouse the values of social work.

It is not within the scope of this chapter to discuss these positions, and I am also aware that the views expressed already could merit closer examination. However, the dilemma is there for everyone. Any explanation of man which sees him as a person having intrinsic dignity and worth – the 'Ethical Man' – must be located in a wider view of the universe and a total reality having its origins in what is personal, or else it will be forced to an intellectual dichotomy.

The humanist must start from an impersonal origin for the universe, because he rejects the existence of a creator. In Zen Buddhism it is said, 'All is God, and there is no God.' There is no distinction between personal and impersonal, and the impersonal comes to cover all that is. Paul Tillich speaks of God as an 'ultimate concern' by which he means anything behind the personality connotation word of 'God'. To the Divine Light Movement 'God' is 'Cosmic Energy' or the 'Primordial Vibration'. The word 'God' may give an illusion of personality to many Western ears but what is meant is impersonal. How can one derive the view that man is a true person, as social work values posit, from any version of the view that there is an impersonal origin to what exists? Practice seems to indicate either that 'Ethical Man' is denied – man being thereby debased or held in philosophical inconsistency with a different view of man. Biblical Christianity, starting from a personal Creator just does not have this problem – it provides a real base for believing that man is of value, and it demands consideration.[26]

Notes

[1] H. M. Bartlett, *The Common Base of Social Work Practice*, NASW, 1970, p.63.

[2] E.J. Thomas (Ed.) *Behavioural Science for Social Workers*, The Free Press, 1967, p.40.

[3] E. Younghusband (Ed.), *Social Work and Social Values*, Allen and Unwin, 1967, p.33.

[4] B.F. Skinner, *Beyond Freedom and Dignity*, Cape, 1972, pp.19, 21.

[5] B.F. Skinner, *Beyond Freedom and Dignity*, p.21.

[6] D. Jehu, P. Hardiker, M. Yellolly and M. Shaw, *Behaviour Modification in Social Work*, Wiley, New York, 1972.

[7] B.F. Skinner, *Beyond Freedom and Dignity*, p.24.

[8] Jehu, Hardiker, Yellolly and Shaw, *Behaviour Modification in Social Work*, p.161.

[9] J. Sandler, C. Dare and A. Holder, *British Journal of Medical Psychology*, June 1972, Vol. 45, Part II.

[10] P. Halmos, *The Faith of the Counsellors*, Constable, 1965 pp. 88, 89.

[11] From *Behaviour Modification in Social Work*, p.163.

[12] K. Marx, *Selected Works*, Vol. I, Foreign Languages Publishing House, Moscow, 1962, pp.362-3 (my italics)

[13] R. Plant, *Social and Moral Theory in Casework*, Routledge and Kegan Paul, 1970, p.11.

14 J.D. Bales, *Communism and the Reality of Moral Law*, Craig Press, New Jersey, USA, 1969.
15 E. Younghusband (Ed.), *Social Work and Social Values*, p.108.
16 John Bowlby, *Maternal Care and Mental Health*, 2nd Edition, Schoken Books, New York, 1966, p.25.
17 R. Plant, *Social and Moral Theory in Casework*, pp.24, 25.
18 I. Goffman, *Asylums*, Penguin, 1961, p.83.
19 C.S. Lewis, *Mere Christianity*, Fontana, 1952, p.31.
20 Francis Schaeffer, *Back to Freedom and Dignity*, Hodder and Stoughton, 1973, p.38.
21 Francis Schaeffer, *True Spirituality*, Hodder and Stoughton, 1972, p.155.
22 J.D. Bales, *Communism and the Reality of Moral Law* pp.50, 51.
23 Halmos, *The Faith of the Counsellors*, p.42.
24 Quoted by H. Prins, 'Motivation in Social Work', *Social Work Today*, 18 April 1974.
25 Francis Schaeffer, *He is There and He is not Silent*, Hodder and Stoughton, 1972, pp.41-2.
26 Parts of the text of this chapter appear in a more extended form in the author's *Social Work's Theory of Man: A New Profession's Philosophical Anthropology*, University of Ulster 1975.

CHAPTER 3

Good Social Organization: Some Hard Questions

John Gladwin

Social workers, along with many others employed by or funded by the state, will be very aware of the profound impact of political and organizational influences upon their work. The capacity to offer the best possible service to members of our community who are living in crisis is affected by these questions of structure. Cuts in expenditure lead to cuts in the service. Poor management leads to an inefficient and unsatisfactory offer of services. Inappropriate political interference undermines professional standards. In situations like these it can be deeply frustrating for those highly trained and highly motivated for giving a service, as they find the opportunities for doing so severely restricted.

Experiences such as these undermine morale in the profession and encourage damaging conflict. Christians share with many others in feeling the pain of the conflicts of loyalties which arise when uncertainty and loss of morale lead to disputes. To whom are we responsible? To our clients, to our political masters, to our colleagues, to ourselves, to God? How do we decide upon such issues? Industrial disputes, periods of radical change of structure and organization, and the threat of loss of resources all raise these hard questions about our duties and responsibilities. These moral questions arise in the midst of the practical decisions confronting us. There is the question about joining a trade union, with the prospect of having to withdraw labour in a dispute. Or the practice of the closed shop. Or how we take collective responsibility within a team, being accountable both to management and to the wider community through its political institutions.

Christian social workers find these questions difficult and, in some cases, are ill-prepared for them. Christianity is often expressed in highly individual and personal terms, and so these questions about trades unions, management and organization can be seen as 'political' rather than 'religious' and so seem to fall outside the terms of Christian belief. But Christian faith does not, of course, tear apart or set in opposition the personal and the social,

41

the full Christian message embraces both and brings them together. There is nothing particularly revolutionary in realising that questions of structure, politics, and social climate have a profound effect upon our individual development and the way we do our job. It is a fact of all human experience. We are deeply influenced by our environment – be it the emotional environment of our family life, or the social environment of our work. These things can contribute to our growth or serve to undermine our vocation. If we are to influence the structure of society through our values and attitudes, we need to recognize their influence and potential effect on us first.

A MATTER OF PRINCIPLE

Let us start by considering the basis of social morality. Are there any principles which undergird healthy social life and organization? If no such values can be found, then the answer to questions of social conduct – should I go on strike? should we accept these changes in lines of accountability? and so on, are merely pragmatic, whatever serves our immediate interest is best. If, however, there are given social values, it is possible to make decisions about what would be the right or wrong thing to do in principle. Such decisions, of course, are always matters of judgement and are open to discussion and amendment as we relate our problems to the principles we believe in. This is why training in moral reasoning is important for Christians working in the profession. Sadly few professional training courses offer much in the way of courses in ethics for social work, neither does the church offer help.

'The image of God'

Christians believe that it is possible to discover some basic values. The first chapter of Genesis tells us that God made us all in his own image and likeness. The more, therefore, we are able to learn about God, the more we can understand the sort of things which help us develop and grow towards the purpose for which we are made. For example, Christians are called to love one another in a similar manner to the way we experience God's love for us. We could soon make a long list of words which capture what we see of God's character revealed supremely in Jesus Christ – mercy, justice, peace, forgiveness, creativity, self-giving, grace... These great words and the truths they picture are like firm boundary posts. In moral discussion we are constantly seeking to discover how these posts link up and provide boundary lines to our conduct. We will return to this moral discussion in a minute.

Basic institutions

The practical outworking of what it means to be made 'in the image of God' is set out in the Bible. The Genesis stories of creation clearly set out basic aspects of human experience in which we see life as God intended it to be for all people. One aspect is our capacity for love and the joy of the bonds of human relationships. This is especially so in the deepest of all relationships – the union of a man and a woman in marriage. Another aspect is the human ability to organize and to rule in the world as part of the vocation God gave to people in the creation stories. We are to order (not destroy) the world and cultivate its life, and we are to be active workers collaborating together in the creative and fruitful use of the resources of the created world. As workers, we are also to learn the harmony of rest, recreation and worship. Thus Christians believe that there are basic institutions given to all of us by God which are appropriate for our life in the world – marriage and family, social and political organizations, work and rest. These institutions take on many and various forms, and the Bible gives us no fixed cultural form. But we are all expected to work to uphold them.

Social workers are only too aware of the way in which aspects of modern life make it difficult for vulnerable people to have a wholesome experience of these institutions. We are continually faced with the damaging effect of poor social provision and values. The disastrous effects of material and emotional poverty (often bound together in a deadly alliance) prevent so many people from finding fulfilment in stable, satisfying and permanent relationships, in making a contribution to the good of others, and in creative fruitful activity in the world. Sadly, the world we live in has been spoilt by human sin and this affects our experience of it. The unjust side of human life in this spoilt world so often leads to one distress piling up on another. The poorer sections of our society are the most vulnerable to unemployment, family stress, ill-health, homelessness, lack of opportunity, restricted choices and early death. All that we do to try and relieve some of these crisis points leads us on to the need for healthier attitudes on the part of every member of the community and to different and better social organization and provision. The whole community has to accept responsibility for the persistence of the ills of poverty, unemployment, and widespread family distress within its midst.

The day-to-day situations which we all face question whether the community really does value the basic institutions of marriage, family, work, and common life in society. The hard facts of experience appear to tell us that we are committed to these things only at a superficial and selfish level. It is at this point that Christianity takes things further, seeing the experience of the poor and bruised not only as something we all share responsibility for, but as a social evil for which we need to discover forgiveness and take action to effect change.

We can, therefore, start our moral comment on structures by questioning forms of social organization and culture which effectively exclude people from the opportunity of experiencing the fundamentals of the created shape of human life. Enforced idleness brought about by unemployment and the inadequate social responses to it is an evil. It is evil because it excludes people from their God-given vocation to creative work. Gross inequality and poverty are evils because they prevent their victims exercising their responsibility, along with others, for managing resources. Poverty undermines family life. It undermines the parental vocation and is a cancer eating at the heart of the bonds of love and mutual dependence. Just as excessive wealth and power corrupt their possessors, so excessive poverty debilitates and prevents people entering their vocation to share in the human experience as God intended it.

In Christian terms, the resolution of these matters involves both a change of heart and values (repentance) and a commitment to find a better way of living together in society (faith and action). Bad social experience is the fruit of bad values and poor institutional provision. Bad social work is often the result of poor values and poor provision in both training and organization.

MAKING DECISIONS

How can we decide what to do? When we are considering reorganization or facing an industrial dispute or working out priorities in the provision of a service, how do we decide? Like any other matters of moral decision, social moral decisions are judgements requiring us to bring a number of different things together. As with anything else, the more we participate and make such judgements the more we build up a fund of experience to help us develop our social conscience and recognize both danger and opportunity.

For Christians there are the following areas to consider:

Christian values

The values we see and experience in Jesus Christ – to love our neighbour as ourself, to love our enemy, to show mercy, practise forgiveness, resist evil, all of which we see in the stories of Jesus in the Gospels – are there to set the standard by which we judge our work.

Accounting for sin

A second important element is to remember human frailty and sinfulness and the realities of life in a fallen world. We strive for a perfection which is still a long way ahead of us. So our decisions will not be perfect and often compromised – making the best we can of the situation we are in. Christians are sometimes frightened off making social decisions because they involve some compromise, but we have to recognize that we cannot attain to perfect love and goodness ourselves. That is why we need the cross – where God through Jesus overcame our evil and offered us reconciliation and hope. We are in regular need of forgiveness and grace to be able to carry on.

Asking questions

The third element concerns asking the right and the hard questions. Questions such as: In whose interests is this proposal? From where does it come? What is it aimed at? What will it involve us in? What will its effects be on our call to serve the vulnerable? What will it do to people? In answering these questions we begin to build up a picture of the social policy under question – be it the aim of a trade union, employer, or of management. When we have the picture we can ask the sharp moral questions: Is the purpose of this good? Are the means acceptable? Will the outcome be worth the investment of effort, conflict, resources?

The answers to our questions may be variable. We may find that although what is being proposed is good – trying to expand the service to meet the needs of a greater range of clients – the means involve added pressure on staff which is not good. Our judgement therefore may be that this proposed reorganization is not acceptable, because its impact on staff will be detrimental to them and ultimately also to the clients. That is an example of social judgement flowing from a moral concern. Within this judgement is found the Christian duty to love, to practise mercy and forgiveness, to resist evil and live in grace and hope.

BALANCING RESPONSIBILITY

Many of the issues concerning social structures and our judgements about them involve conflicts of interests. This can be seen at all sorts of levels. There are always many more needs to be met than resources to match them. It isn't always possible to serve the interests of everyone to whom we owe a responsibility – the different groups of our clients, our colleagues, management, the wider community of the profession. Even so, these are just the groups thought of from a work point of view. We might also mention our responsibility to our family, our church, our neighbours, and even to ourselves. And all this is to be seen within and under our responsibility to God.

The art of good social organization is to bring these levels of responsibility into as much harmony as is possible. Situations in which we are forced to choose between responsibilities – as, for example, in the event of an industrial dispute – are symptomatic of deeper failures in the organization to hold levels of responsibility together. If it is at all possible we are to live at peace with all people – a peace that can be promoted by good social arrangements and hindered by poor ones. Good systems of communication, clearly-defined boundaries of responsibility, appropriate roles, flexibility in relationships all assist an organization to function humanly and peaceably and provide the basis for the doing of good tasks in the wider community.

The question, 'Who, or what, is responsible for this situation?' is crucial to serious moral reflection. In social work, as in other professional practice, we have learnt to avoid burdening individuals with the full responsibility for circumstances beyond their immediate control. In general, we do not blame the poor for their poverty. The answer to poverty does not lie in exhorting poor people to make greater efforts at succeeding. The greater burden of responsibility lies with the wider community who have a duty to provide against the effects of involuntary poverty. A combination of better social values, public commitment to action, and better public policies can provide an environment within which the poor can assume greater responsibility and choice over their own living. Only when we meet our collective responsibilities can individuals be helped to assume theirs when their situation has been created to large measure by a failure of corporate policy.

Frequently, the answer to the question about responsibility is multiple. In an industrial dispute, for example, it is usually possible to identify a range of failures in responsibility all contributing to the conflict. At the individual level there may have been a failure to take any interest in the developing dispute, non-attendance at union meetings, and a failure to exercise an opinion. At a collective level management may have failed to maintain sufficient communication to be able to understand the point of view of the work-force. The trade union may have been slack and failed to act soon enough to enable a peaceful resolution of difference. The political authorities may have contributed by making decisions in what appeared to be an arbitrary manner. It is only when we discuss and analyze in a detailed manner that we can seriously arrive at understanding the different levels of responsibility. When such a picture is available the moral test is in the capacity of individuals, groups and organizations to accept responsibility and act accordingly.

When Christians are trying to work out the nature of their attitude towards, and responsibility for, social structures, they are really trying to draw up a moral map for the social context. For this, information of an accurate and agreed nature is vital. Then some guidelines are needed by which the material can be assembled and interpreted. Gradually a picture emerges, helping the reader to see the choices available. We try to plot a good and hopeful route forward on the map, to make the journey successfully may involve building new bridges, repairing old structures, and using well-tried and tested paths and routes. By such means Christians act as messengers of the Gospel – the good news of Jesus Christ – helping others to see something of the care and love God has for his world and our experience of it.

Our experience of the immediate social work context is a mirror of the wider needs of society. Christians have a strong interest in making and maintaining peaceful life in society, which depends on a commitment to justice and an acknowledgement of a common life shared with other members of the community. This is why it is a failure if Christians retire to their corner to carry on 'good works' in isolation. Christian social workers have a duty to the organization of the profession and from that to the organization of our social order, which is responsible not only for the provision of the service we offer, but also, to a degree, for the conditions of life which give rise to our work. The presence of the poor, the vulnerable, and the deprived are a testimony to poor social values and inadequate provision throughout our society. There can be no serious progress if these major structural social issues are not addressed. Christian social workers have a part to play in helping us all meet our obligations and accept our responsibilities.

CHAPTER 4

The Political Imperative

Terry Drummond
Katherine Mundy

A key question for Christians in social work is the relationship of faith to political action. On the one hand there are those who believe that faith is about individual salvation and that religion is essentially private; on the other there are those whose commitment is to a gospel of political action. It is particularly important for Christians involved in social work to consider the issues of personal faith and public action in terms of a biblical, historical and theological approach. Out of these will emerge an approach to society that shows Christianity to be relevant to people's needs, and seeking to work for a system of care that responds to contemporary social needs.

What follows is based on our understanding that politics is the whole area of concern relating to the involvement of the state with our individual lives. As a starting-point for discussion, we believe that for Christians an understanding of a political approach must begin with a biblical understanding of our relationship to the state. In order to provide the context for the coming of Jesus and his concern for the poor, we must begin with the relationship of New Testament teaching to its origins in the Old Testament, in the people of Israel. They were a nation with a clear political understanding. Although in course of time they had kings, their ultimate king was God. They were under his rule. The laws as laid out in the books of Leviticus and Deuteronomy are both complex and interesting. Particularly important in the context of political attitudes is their approach to the outcast and the alien, orphans, widows and immigrants.

The most important truth for the people of Israel was that they were under the supreme direction of God and answerable solely to him. The laws were based on this understanding: to disobey them was to disobey God. The laws reflect a God who is clearly on the side of the poor and the oppressed and who demands justice. The Jubilee Law in Leviticus in which, every fiftieth year, land was to be restored to its original owner, freedom and property to be restored, shows a concern for all the people – the poor, the slaves and other aliens. It reminded the people that the land belonged to

God, and stopped the wealthy from exploiting the poor. Although this law was never enacted, it was clearly laid down. In the later period the prophets were clearly called to bring the people back to obedience to God's law. Their message for those who ill-treat the poor is one of condemnation.

Amos says: 'They sell into slavery honest men who cannot pay their debts, poor men who cannot repay even the price of a pair of sandals. They trample down the weak and helpless and push the poor out of the way.'[1]

Isaiah says: 'You are doomed! You make unjust laws that oppress my people. That is how you prevent the poor from getting justice. That is how you take the property that belongs to widows and orphans.'[2]

These are only two examples of many that can be found in the writings of the prophets where the message is one of condemnation for the misuse of wealth. The political imperative is to return to God and in so doing to destroy all injustice and oppression.

The New Testament message, as found in the Gospels, follows the same tradition. Jesus came as the culmination of the history of God's people. He came to bring salvation (wholeness) to each individual with a message that challenged the Jewish leaders and those who misinterpreted the law. Christians see Jesus as a spiritual teacher and leader which he clearly was. But within his teaching there is also a direct political message. When he proclaimed his Kingdom by reading words from the prophet Isaiah in the synagogue in Nazareth, he identified with the prophet's message of 'good news for the poor and release for the captives'.[3]

Some Christians see this message from the perspective of a 'bias to the poor', but we can see that the counterbalance is a bias *against* the rich and the misuse of wealth. For Jesus shows us that wealth can make it hard for people to follow God. Greed and possessiveness harden the heart; generosity and justice bring freedom. When Jesus met the rich young ruler who wanted to follow him, he told him: 'One thing you still lack. Sell all that you have and distribute to the poor and you will have treasure in heaven and come follow me.'[4] The Gospel records that the man became sad, because he was very rich. 'How hard it is for rich people to enter the Kingdom of God!' Jesus said.

If we read the Gospels in the light of this teaching, we will find Jesus clearly calling people to repentance, with a message that includes the condemnation of the misuse of wealth, expressed in failing to care for those in society who have no power – the poor, the outcast, the widows and the orphans.

The political imperative in these texts challenges Christians in every age to take seriously the needs of the poor and those who are outcasts of society. Equally, it is based on an understanding that Jesus himself, in taking humanity through his incarnation, was actually prepared to show the way forward. As Sara Maitland says:

'The humanity of Jesus means the solidarity and identification of all Christians, not just with each other, but more importantly with all oppressed, enslaved people.'[5]

Jesus, the Son of God, turned the world's standards upside down, becoming powerless and weak, yet with a call to justice, mercy, and self-giving love. He condemns the Pharisees who could keep parts of the law, but failed to stand by the poor, and affirmed the 'good news' that the poor are truly people loved by God who deserve to be recognized and given their full worth.

This message of the New Testament is one that has been explored throughout the church's history. In this century, Third World theologians, those of Latin America in particular, offer guidance, support and understanding of a message that places the poor in the forefront of the struggle for justice. In our richer, Western society we do not see this same concern. We ourselves believe that while the ethical and traditional theological problems are important, the matter of how we treat those with no material wealth is a pressing concern.

We need more faith to take a political stance based on the teaching found in the Gospels and so to understand the contemporary issues in the light of Jesus' teaching. Using the Gospels as our starting-point, we would place equal stress on the importance of the incarnation – God identifying with his people as a suffering servant, Jesus, who was not only king, but also man who came to elevate all people to share in that same kingship. In these terms the Kingdom of God becomes real – God's involvement with the *whole* of our lives, including the political dimension.

This message is one that transcends history. The early Church Fathers clearly saw the role of Christians to be one of sharing all they had, and throughout the church's history groups have tried to move towards a concern for the outcast. The first hospitals and organized care for the outcast were an expression of Christian concern.

In Britain the development of urban society in the nineteenth century brought with it the early social work agencies – Barnardo's, The Salvation Army, The Charity Organization Society. All had their basis in the Christian faith and many grew out of a concern for individual salvation and conversion. Though most did not take an overtly political role, they attempted to serve the poor with practical care. On the political side there was the work of the Clapham Sect, men such as Wilberforce and Shaftesbury, who used their wealth and influence to create better laws and standards. The leaders of the Oxford Movement, usually thought of as ritualists, also had a burning concern for the poor:

> 'Dr Pusey certainly possessed a powerful belief that the poor, as well as the rich, were members of Christ's body. He was, therefore, appalled that one Christian lady could "wear as one of her manifold dresses, which would have removed the growing hunger of some 7,000 members of CHRIST"!'[6]

The priests and religious workers of the movement went to serve in areas of immense social deprivation and many sought to challenge injustice – for example, poor housing, sanitation, or poverty. Most important, their concern arose out of sacramental worship and an understanding of the incarnation.

The clarification of these issues in contemporary theological thinking is found in the work of the Latin American liberation theologians, who offer a criteria for action:

> 'For it is not possible to struggle against injustice and yet not analyse the causes of injustice and possible ways of dealing with them.'[7]

> 'Poverty is a social sin that God does not will and so there is an urgent obligation to change things to help fellow human beings and to act in obedience to God.'[8]

The task for Christian social workers is summed up in the writings of these men and women which point to a political imperative that takes seriously the poor and the needy. It is based on the most important of all Christian truths – that we are called to be disciples of Jesus, and that will cost, in T.S. Eliot's words: 'Not less than everything.'

To follow the Jesus of the Gospels is to face the powers of society head-on and show that Christians will not absolve the evil that surrounds them. The casework role of the social worker in 'binding wounds' is important and will be carried on. But it will not be all that is done, for out of this will arise a movement for political action. In our opinion, the Christian faith has for too long been used to justify Christian individualism where the battle is confined to individual sin. In a society where we see the poor being treated as a 'non-people' and the acceptance of growing unemployment sin must be seen as the evil which surrounds us all. No Christian, least of all one involved in social work, can afford not to take these issues seriously. So what can we do to work for fundamental change?

WORKING FOR CHANGE

The changing face of British society and, in particular, the problems being faced by the welfare state must lead to a consideration of how Christians can and should respond. The growth of poverty and unemployment and the related problems lead to the questions: 'What do we say to those with power?' and 'What can we offer to the disadvantaged?' If we are to take our mandate from the life of Jesus and the biblical imperative of concern for the outcast, then there is an obvious Christian challenge to fight on behalf of the deprived.

Two recent commentators had this to say on the state of current welfare policy in Britain:

'Clearly welfare capitalism is beset by problems, economic, social and political. The authority and capacity of Government to solve the problems which confront them are being questioned. Government no longer seems able to draw on any of Weber's classic sources of legitimacy, tradition, charisma, or rationality and legality. The era of consensus politics and near universal support for the mixed economy and the welfare state is over. Students emphasize increasingly the degree to which the welfare state was a product of a peculiar coincidence of circumstances, a post-war state of solidarity, economic growth, Keynesian principles of economic management, a confidence in Government's ability to right wrongs. Now the stress is all on the way the welfare state has failed in its central objectives, the reduction of inequality, the abolition of poverty, the forging of a new social unity; more is spent, but problems survive. Issues of welfare have become less important to voters; there is a sense that enough has been done...'[9]

If these are the issues at stake then Christian social workers have a commitment to finding a solution to how we best enable growth for the most disadvantaged. The social worker with a heavy caseload within a dwindling service can be involved only in a form of care based on crisis intervention rather than prevention. This will lead inevitably to the stretching of personal and spiritual resources, resulting in personal deprivation in the form of 'burn-out'. In itself this may be a way of ensuring that little criticism is levelled at a system that condones the immorality of economic decline that allows the growth of poverty and unemployment to continue unchecked and which may lead to other social problems, such as non-accidental injury, alcoholism, drug addiction, and so on.

The churches have at a central level various bodies that are immediately concerned to challenge these changing standards – the Anglican boards of social responsibility and the equivalent organizations within other denominations – but as centralized bodies their power is limited and they have little to offer a social worker who will be facing the issues day-to-day. Equally, the development of a group such as Church Action on Poverty, or its secular equivalent, Child Poverty Action Group, cannot offer a wide net of support for the grass roots worker. These are national campaigns and will be restricted to those with time to give.

Christian social workers should be in touch with the organizations that are prepared to offer support – where possible giving advice on issues. But to be effective we believe the Christian social worker must get to work in the local context. The national battle is an important one, but change may be easier to effect if pursued at local level. The real challenge is to establish work which will meet the long-term needs of the disadvantaged. So often social work is about offering immediate assistance, or possibly being an advocate for the client, both of which are important. But an equally important task is to assist the disadvantaged in different areas to establish their own self-help projects. The poor do not lack leadership skills, they more often lack the confidence to use them. A major task is to affirm the local leaders and help them to find their own place. Encouraging self-help may assist the needy to be their own advocates.

The implications of the decline of the welfare state are daunting. Change must come through support at local levels. Change will not be brought about by attacking the *status quo* with academic arguments, but rather by finding ways to make changes, presenting the evidence of poverty and finding ways of changing attitudes. The challenge for the Christian social worker is to take up the message of Amos and the other prophets, to show that the poor must not be overridden. The inevitable clash with elected members and government must be faced. People with strong political motivation are prepared to take on the battle; we believe Christians must be prepared to do the same.

The whole Christian gospel shows us that Jesus is not just a spiritual guide offering hope at death, but the one who gives hope to change the world, just as he has made forgiveness and new life possible for any individual. Christians have no less a task in front of them than to change the society in which they live. The road that lies ahead is a hard one; it is always a challenge:

> 'The solidarity required by the preferential option for the poor forces us back to a fundamental Christian attitude: a grasp of the need for continual conversion. We are then able to find in the break with former ways and in our chosen new way deeper dimensions of a personal and social, material and spiritual kind. The conversion to the Lord to which solidarity with the oppressed brings us calls for stubbornness and constancy on the road we have undertaken.'[10]

The challenge for British social workers who call themselves Christian is to be open to continual conversion and change. Then faith becomes not a cosy fall-back, but rather a challenge to see the possibility of a new society. For some this attitude may be seen as a new way and we hope that those who come to it fresh will take on the challenge.

But political action must not be divorced from prayer and faith. All Christians need to begin from their own spiritual starting-point, be that a prayer meeting or the Eucharist, where all men and women, rich and poor, meet as one in Christ. Our prayer must be the starting-point for action. In the incarnation of Jesus we see God for our sakes prepared to share our earthly life. Our task is to live a life like his and be willing to go into the world and to seek change. He is there before us, and change is possible – but only if we seek it in the knowledge that we love and worship a God who identifies with our humanity.

Notes

[1] Amos 2:6,7a, Good News Bible.
[2] Isaiah 10:1,2, Good News Bible.
[3] Luke 4:18,19.
[4] Luke 18:18-29.
[5] Sara Maitland, *Map of a New Country*, Routledge and Kegan Paul 1983, p.14.

[6] James Bentley, 'Dr Marx and Dr Pusey', *After Marx*, Jubilee Publications, 1984, p.20.
[7] Gustavo Gutierrez, *We Drink from our own Wells*, SCM Press 1984, p.107.
[8] Leonardo Boff, *Jesus Christ, Liberator*, Maryknoll, New York, p.270.
[9] Vic George and Paul Wilding, *The Impact of Social Policy*, Routledge and Kegan Paul, 1984, pp.246-47.
[10] See note 7 above.

CHAPTER 5

Christianity and the Psychodynamic Approach

Andrew Henderson

The significance of Jesus Christ cannot be divorced from the historical context of his life. The civilized world of that time and the cultures within it were ready for a transformation of the understanding of God's relationship to the world and to human beings. Some Christians feel that even to point this out takes away from the divinity of Jesus. Others believe that the more our understanding of his significance is naturalized the more authentic is the interpretation of the incarnation, the good news that God came down to earth from heaven.

PARALLEL REFLECTIONS

The teachings and insights of Freud emerged in a world already struggling to hold together the traditional religious and meta-physical understandings of the human spirit and personality with the implications of a more scientific approach to life in all its aspects. The western world was ready for Freud and it did not take many decades for the effects of his work to percolate through to every sphere of interpersonal work.

Psychoanalysis impinged on social work first through child guidance clinics, and then mainly through the drive to improve standards of training and care in work with children and their families. Many of us, struggling to find meaning for our own lives as well as for our clients, must be tantalized in one form or another by the possibility that the language of Christianity and that of psychoanalytic understanding may in fact be talking about the same things. Is there so much difference between salvation and integration; between revelation and insight?

THE PSYCHODYNAMIC APPROACH

Most people have a clear idea of what is meant by the word 'Christianity', they may distinguish between the faith and 'going to church' but, by and large, the story of the birth, life, death and resurrection of Jesus Christ is a distinguishing mark that sets the religious faith apart from humanistic philosophy.

Psychoanalysis, like Christianity, has spawned many sub-groups and sects, often characterized by the venom with which they insist that they and they alone are the repository of the 'true faith'. When it comes to social work practice, many analysts would deny that the sort of therapeutic enterprise undertaken in social casework can claim any true connection with psychoanalysis. Nevertheless, there is now a strong tradition in social work derived from psychoanalytic thought which is often called 'the psychodynamic approach'.

For the purpose of this chapter that phrase stands for two tenets in combination:

First: that the human personality is formed developmentally through social interaction, so that all previous experience, and especially formative early experience, affects present behaviour;

Second: that the conscious mind is only one facet of the full personality – so that any attempt to promote beneficial change must have due regard to unconscious and subconscious elements.

People who do not like social work criticize it as interfering and pretentious. Barbara Wootton opined that 'social workers... present themselves to the world... deeply tainted with what Virginia Woolf has called "the peculiar repulsiveness of those who dabble their fingers self-approvingly in the stuff of other's souls".'[1] But it is clear that given the territory of human distress that social workers move in (indeed are statutorily obliged to occupy), they are dealing with issues that not so long ago would have been recognized as spiritual.

Although daunting at first, the acceptance of at least an element of the work of a 'doctor of souls' in all interpersonal transactions is liberating and is now buttressed by a great range of writing that sets out to reconcile traditional Christian beliefs with psychodynamic insights. H.A. Williams has written bravely and brilliantly from his own experience in a whole series of books and Christopher Bryant's *The River Within* is a convincing presentation of depth psychology for the Christian.[2]

What is meant by the 'psychodynamic approach' looks like an attempt to address human beings in their physical and spiritual entirety.

FOR MYSELF OR FOR MY CLIENT?

The connection between social work and psychoanalysis is at its clearest in psychoanalytically based casework and group work. In certain specialized settings a social worker may be a member of a team whose members all equally share in psychotherapeutic activity. Occasionally the social worker may in fact be a psychotherapist, having undertaken a personal analysis or training. Some day centres and some residential units, especially those for children and those recovering from mental illness, have analytically based programmes using the techniques of group analysis and regression therapy.

However, the major influence of psychoanalysis on social work is much more generalized: first, through the extent to which such thinking is now commonly received into the educational upbringing of everyone in our culture; and second, through students in training absorbing a sort of *lingua franca* that incorporates the basic psyschodynamic insights outlined above. This is important in order to form a basis of understanding and communication between workers within an agency, and also for ease of communication across agency and professional boundaries. What is more tendentious is the extent to which such an approach should be offered to clients as well as informing the activities of the workers. For instance, insight-giving techniques, once popular amongst social work practitioners, are now recognized to be of limited value with many social services clients who, because of the social remit to a local authority department to act as an agency of last resort, may be too fragile to benefit from such an approach. (You have to be fairly well to use psychoanalysis and the same goes for the related activity in social work.)

This is analogous to the position of the worker who is sustained by a personal commitment to the Christian gospel and who may make constant internal reference to the values which flow from this commitment, without making them explicit to his or her clients. Often such a commitment is not generally shared with colleagues either, and in this it differs from the psychoanalytic base of much interpersonal social work. Whereas our society has withdrawn common consent from Christian interpretations as the assured base for the whole of activity at home and at work, the core psychoanalytic beliefs in the importance of early life experiences and in something that is conveniently described as 'the unconscious' are now widely held and certainly have become underlying assumptions in the practice of the social work agencies.

Just as with religious commitment and values, so with psychodynamic understandings, the profile they hold in the believer's 'conscious' mind may be high or low. Many of us do not consciously check back to our beliefs of either sort. Probably most of us absorb the basis of our values without realizing it is happening and thereafter act instinctively and intuitively in line with those values once our 'spiritual computer' has been programmed. Perhaps the key value that bridges Christian and psychodynamic approaches is the respect for the integrity of each individual, and the importance of striving for each individual's full development and wholeness. Whether or not we articulate that in so many words, if it is what we believe, we can be sure that it is what we communicate to our clients.

SPEAKING PICTURES

While no one doubts that the Christian faith is based on the historical events of the life of Jesus, many Christians nowadays are sympathetic with a view that credal beliefs use historical facts to express and to illustrate aspirations, dreams and commitments that go to the heart of human nature and the meaning of life.

So too with the pictures of human personality offered by psychoanalysis: no one actually believes that the personality is like an iceberg floating in the sea of the collective unconscious, or that the mind is layered like a neopolitan icecream, with the ego and the id lurking at different levels. These are convenient and powerful pictures to express the beliefs that guide our approach to our work.

When the psychoanalytic view of human beings crystallized through the work of Freud, the dominant and official expositions of Christian belief were still expressed chiefly in a literal interpretation of the biblical stories. Even though analytic theories were not truly verifiable by scientific method, they *appeared* to be opposed to the metaphysical beliefs of Christianity and aligned with the experiential approach of science.

Since then Christianity and the churches have moved rapidly in an amoeba-like fashion to absorb and to incorporate the new understandings and to rediscover in the traditions of Christian mysticism the primeval insistence of people of faith that true humanity and the Divine are paradoxically both different and the same. John Robinson used an exciting phrase 'the beyond within' to convey this new understanding in *Honest to God*.[3]

Clearly the work of Jung offers a general way into reconciling religious traditions with psychoanalytic understandings. But if we are to home in on what is specifically Christian, the central figure of Christ rising from the dead is what work with loss and separation is all about and of course psychoanalysis has its own pictures about that too. The basic human experience is the same. There is a connection between loss and new beginnings; between loss and death; between grieving and new life; between suffering and its transformation.

WHAT FAITH/BELIEF UNDERLIES SOCIAL WORK?

Helping activity can be underpinned by any number of theoretical frameworks which guide interaction between helper and helped. Some practitioners believe in techniques centred on interpersonal transaction, while others focus on political intervention or on the manipulation of significant external factors. Yet what is common to all these approaches is a certain shared fundamental belief in the validity, importance and effectiveness of love. Some may shy away from the use of such a word, but the best practitioners and managers of social worker and social services, the ones who command the instinctive respect of colleagues and clients, are those who convey that they are free enough in themselves to attend to the real problems and pain of the client; that they believe in the inherent resources of the client to work and to own their decisions. Such people can convey that they respect their clients enough to help them to face unpalatable aspects of themselves and their behaviour, and that while doing all this they will not desert them. They show that they are willing to take over when necessary, if only for a time, and can confirm rather than take away the humanity of their clients. If this is not loving, it is difficult to know what is. Tough loving, yes, and loving for which we are paid, but true loving.

All this connects up very directly with the Christian exaltation of love – 'faith, hope and love; there are these three and the greatest of these is love' and is beautifully related to counselling in *Illusion and Reality* by David Smail.[4]

The emergence of the analytic understanding of human beings assists true loving by offering a way of self-understanding which does justice to our experience of ourselves. Chaotic, contradictory and destructive urges fit into the picture of the unconscious areas of personality, and the perception that the past lives on in the present helps to free us from the need to externalize the explanation of pain and suffering into metaphysical beliefs in devils and demons. The psychoanalytic understanding contributes the possibility of a mature stance in the face of evil. Rather than perceiving ourselves as the weak victims of a cosmic struggle between gods and demigods we can connect with a vision, however dim, of ourselves as participant creators through our choices and decisions however circumscribed these may be.

FAITH AND WORKS

Christian theology has always seen a tension between faith and works. The clear biblical teaching is that the salvation of the human soul is achieved by faith in the saving action of God through Christ. And faith is a gift from God which we cannot finally secure by our own efforts. Our part is to create the conditions in our lives which are most likely to nurture this gift. The story of Martha, from the Gospels, illustrates this beautifully. Martha is busy, bustling about, to entertain Jesus and his friends. She appeals to Jesus to tell her sister Mary to help her. Mary is paying rapt attention to the arresting words of their visitor. 'No,' says Jesus. 'Mary has chosen the better part.' Yet he also asked in another context, 'Do you gather figs from thorns or grapes from thistles? You will know them by their fruits.' Faith without effective action is dead, but faith comes first.

The very phrase 'social work' has an activist connotation, but the listening ear is also central to psychoanalytic and psychotherapeutic methods, and the belief that true healing has to come from within undergirds the non-directive approach in counselling. True, it is complemented by ego-strengthening techniques and by the specific use of authoritative direction in some circumstances, but 'helping people to help themselves' has always been central to the social work approach. Rather than taking over the control of clients' lives, social work tries to help people to be more in charge of themselves and their circumstances. This approach presupposes that human beings, whatever their current dysfunction, have the latent ability to develop towards wholeness and independence.

It would be surprising if such high ideals were always realized. There is a rather exquisite parallel between the impatience many Christians feel with the church and the critical feelings many dynamically-oriented social work professionals direct towards their social service departments. Just as many sincere Christians feel that the church has compromised too deeply with this imperfect world and has emasculated the radical nature of the gospel in order to preserve its institutional interests, so many social services staff would like to see social work stand for a reassertion of the primacy of human needs over the demands of our systems. It sometimes seems that the bureaucracies of the Welfare State are more concerned with control than with care, and more anxious to defend their own existence than to foster health change.

BRINGING IN THE KINGDOM: SALVATION AND INTEGRATION

In Jewish biblical theology there is little room for the notion of an individual person achieving his own salvation apart from the perfection of the whole of society – the people of God. The New Testament develops the theme into the new community of those who the Holy Spirit in which Christians are created, formed and sustained by their interaction with each other follow Christ. At first sight classic psychoanalysis might seem to contradict this and to reinforce an individualistic approach: the picture of the single patient on the couch hour after hour suggests that. But to complement that came the new understanding of the importance of parenthood and of the group, and the social context of human development – in fact the whole corpus of social studies which form the background for social work practice.

It is this central experience of life as a conversation between the individual and the community which links Christian belief and spirituality so clearly to the values of social work and social services. God saved the world by becoming human. That is the nub of the Christian faith, taking the special relationship with God into the heart of everyone. The implications of this faith are that as members one with another, none of us can claim personal fulfilment and completion until the saving work of God brings the New Jerusalem for all.

As for the Christian believer, so for those working within a psychodynamic understanding of life, there can be no escape from the significance of every decision and action, not just for ourselves but for the world we live in. Lasting change, the freeing, the integration and healing of the human psyche will come about not so much through the decisions of governments, as through the changing of individual hearts, each one a microcosm of the whole.

Notes

[1] Barbara Wootton, *Social Science and Social Pathology*, Allen & Unwin, 1959.
[2] Christopher Bryant, *The River Within*, Darton, Longman and Todd, 1978.
[3] SCM Press, 1962.
[4] David Smail, *Illusion and Reality*, J.M. Dent & Son, 1984.

PART 2

The Christian Social Worker in Practice

CHAPTER 6

Working in the Community

Bob Holman

Mondays at 8.30 a.m. I unlock the doors of the Southdown
Community Project and attempt to avoid being trampled
underfoot by the youngsters who rush in. After a hectic half hour
of snooker, darts and table tennis, I chase them to school. The
week has started and for seven days the centre will be used by
mothers' groups, the elderly, youth clubs and a community association. The project's four workers also help individuals with housing, financial and delinquency difficulties. The children and adults
are drawn from a collection of council houses known as
Southdown. It is these people and this place which I regard as the
community served by the project.

The project was established in 1976. It is not a community work
agency which concentrates on stimulating collective action. Rather
it is a community social work body which offers services to the
neighbourhood. As such it may appear similar to a local authority
centre. But there is a difference. The project is sponsored by a
Christian voluntary society, the Church of England Children's
Society, and the project's team has attempted to apply Christian
insights to their work.

CHRISTIANS AND THE COMMUNITY

Why are Christians developing services in a community? The
straightforward answer is that they believe in making a contribution towards the kind of society God wants on earth. In the Bible,
the family emerges as a God-given institution which provides love,
nurture and protection. But the family is never isolated from the
needs of others and members are also expected to embrace the
stranger, the foreigner, the outcast. When Jesus Christ came to
earth, he was not content merely to state the twin values of family
and individual. He activated them. He chose to be part of a family
yet also sought to befriend outsiders. Moreover, he established the
virtues of mercy and love which should guide personal and social
relationships.

Jesus therefore made clear the kind of kingdom that should exist

65

on earth. But the kingdom has yet to be completed. Meanwhile, it is evident that personal and structural evils result in deprivations and distress for multitudes. The victims are the people for whom Christians should have a special concern. In the Old Testament, God frequently instructed his people to care for the oppressed. When God's Son came to earth, he identified with the poor and later declared that his mission was to give priority to the poor. It is amongst the same people that today's Christians should be most prepared to promote the well-being of families and individuals.

The above statement is a crude explanation of why Christians in particular should be involved in upholding certain values in low-income neighbourhoods. Such considerations took hold of my life when I was an academic in the 1970s. I felt that my abilities – such as they were – should not be concentrated on a university. Simultaneously, I was concerned at the plight of the family, particularly at the numbers of delinquent and deprived children who were being taken away from poor parents. Soon after, I met Dave Wiles, a former delinquent, whose conversion to Christianity sparked off a desire to do something useful on the estate where he had been raised, the very council estate which was attracting my attention. The result was the initiation of the Southdown Community Project with the aims of preventing children being taken from their families, of working with 'at risk' youngsters and providing facilities for the community. The project, which started with one worker in my house, now employs four full-timers based at that building where youngsters pile in each morning.

A CHRISTIAN APPROACH

Initiating a project and defining aims is fairly straightforward. Deciding how to attain objectives is much more complicated. Gradually the team members have hewn out an approach which owes something to the Christian concepts of servanthood, oneness and togetherness.

God referred to Jesus as 'my servant' in the prophecy of Isaiah, and quoted in Matthew's Gospel. The same Jesus refused to be crowned King, washed the disciples' feet and exhorted them to do likewise. The concept of *servanthood* does not mean weakness. Jesus had a mission and would allow nothing to stop him. Being a servant entails a readiness to accept a lowly position, to take into account the needs of others and to sacrifice one's own interests.

Jesus shocked his contemporaries by insisting on the *oneness* or equality before God of all people. When he conversed with women, touched lepers and welcomed foreigners he was acting radically. He insisted that not only should fishermen, thieves and revolutionaries be allowed to join his followers, but also that they took on tasks of leadership. Thus barriers of class and race were broken down.

And, in time, the oneness of Jesus' followers became a *togetherness*. There developed a sense of what the New Testament calls fellowship as people discovered how to live with and even die for each other.

Before describing the attempt to apply these concepts to the project, two qualifications must be made. First, Jesus was not setting out a social work blueprint. Nonetheless, I feel it is legitimate to consider the implications of his teachings for social work as for any other aspect of living. Second, other factors also influenced the approaches which we adopted. A critique of current social work practice was one. For instance, a decision that project workers should live in the neighbourhood sprang from the perception that the impact of statutory social workers was weakened by the distance of their residences and offices from the people they were intended to help. Again, the Christian desire to side with the poor and to promote togetherness had much in common with socialist ideas of equality and fraternity. This overlap between Christian thinking, social work analysis and socialist principles is difficult to disentangle. All that can be added is that I would have been reluctant to pursue any social work or socialist paths which led away from Christianity.

Given the strong part played by Christianity, the question is sometimes asked 'What right have you to be so specifically Christian?' One reason is that the project is part of a Christian agency whose voluntary funds are donated by people sympathetic to Christian values. More important, the right depends on neighbourhood approval of what the project does and stands for. The team would pack up if local support did not exist. Happily, the project does seem to possess such backing. Indeed, the proposal for a project building and the resulting fund-raising efforts derived from residents' initiatives.

IN PRACTICE

Having explained the background to the community project, the rest of this chapter will concentrate on describing how the Christian concepts were applied. This will cover the practice of the workers, their reaction to failures and criticisms, their attitude to collective action, and their direct expression of Christianity.

If Christ's teaching about servanthood, oneness and togetherness were taken seriously, then the effects should be evident in the manner in which the project carries out its tasks. The following items seem most relevant:

First, the idea of serving others implies a *readiness to listen* to what people request. The opening three months of the project were spent door-knocking. Neighbours' grumbles about children running wild in the streets and youngsters' complaints about boredom, led to the start of a youth club. Subsequent requests for play schemes, mothers' groups, a keep fit class, holidays, football teams and so on, were usually accepted provided they fitted in with the aims of the project.

Second, a servant is *available*. Consequently, the project is open on evenings and weekends and not restricted to the weekday hours of 9 a.m. to 5 p.m. Occasionally, it is dramatic, as when a teenager burst into my home late one Saturday desperate for drugs or glue. Sometimes it is amusing as when, one evening, a boy rushed in for refuge convinced that mum was about to implement a threat to cut off his ear if he wore an ear-ring – in fact, his donning the ring had coincided with mum picking up a large pair of scissors to do dressmaking. Most often, availability means a succession of low-key calls from people who are bored, depressed or want to borrow something.

Third, serving entails doing *practical, useful tasks for others*. For instance, when a father was devastated by the desertion of his wife, one of the project team, Jane Sellars, undertook to clean his house until he felt able to cope. When a lone mother had to enter hospital, the team looked after her children so as to avoid them having to go into local authority care. If children cannot afford a holiday, it is usually possible to take them along on the project's camps and vacations.

Fourth, the desire to promote oneness and togetherness has made *local involvement* a major part of day-to-day practice. A users' committee has recently been established, but most emphasis has been placed on recruiting residents to be paid volunteers, trainee leaders and full-time workers. Nine residents are paid small fees to help run the clubs and groups. Each year, six local teenagers are appointed to one activity, expected to keep a diary and attend training sessions and, if successful, receive a youth leader's certificate. A previously unemployed girl has now been taken on a two year full-time contract. A permanent full-timer is Jim Davis who has spent all his life on the estate. Not least, Dave Wiles has now taken over as project leader. Thus, both the leadership and daily routine of the project is rooted in the community.

Such involvement brings advantages. Without it, the project could not cope with the large numbers who attend. Further, the locals often bring great skills. Dave Wiles, with his own knowledge of delinquency and rapport with teenagers, is better at the job than I am. But, in addition, participation supports the Christian values of the project. For instance, nobody is barred because of their background or record. I have just left a hectic youth club attended by seventy children. Coping with them was a man made redundant in his sixties, a boy recently convicted of a serious theft, a middle-aged local mum, three lone mothers, a teenager with truancy problems and several other youngsters. The inclusion of such a range of people promotes a sense of oneness.

The involvement of the unemployed, the delinquent, the low-income adult – in short, the kind of people often thought of as outsiders – serves a Christian purpose in yet another way. God has made people with the capacity and need to give as well as to receive. Indeed, in the Acts of the Apostles, Paul recalls that Jesus said 'It is more blessed to give than to receive'. One of the dangers of modern social work – from the best of intentions – is a tendency to do things *to* or *for* people. The deserted dad, the depressed mum, the young offender thus find they are treated just as recipients. The result is not only to confirm an image of them as problem people, but also to deny them the opportunity to contribute. Hopefully, the inclusion of such people in the 'oneness' of the project helps to make them the whole or full kind of person God intended.

Not least, the demonstration that ordinary people possess the skills to maintain a community project demolishes the myth that helping is the preserve of professional experts. The consequence of this appears to be a greater confidence in offering aid both inside and outside the project. When a working couple lost the woman who met and cared for their child after school, the self-run mothers' group took them in and found a replacement. Another group, which originated at the project, has developed a network outside with members supporting and caring for each other. In these ways, a sense of mutual responsibility, of togetherness, is growing.

Fifth, the project workers have given some thought to the *implications of Christian concepts to themselves as a team*. For instance, the trend in social work agencies towards management hierarchies, emphasis on status and salary differences, and rigid distinctions of roles seems at odds with notions of fellowship, humility and oneness. The project tries to diminish these differences. Staff do not have separate offices or desks. The team meets together to allocate work and consult with each other. All members take on a range of tasks – running clubs, organizing camps, counselling individuals, liaising with outside bodies, and so on. Any confusion and overlap is compensated by an ability to do each others' jobs in times of crisis or illness and a great sense of unity. An attempt to share out the cleaning jobs has failed because one person insists on doing most of it! Above all, the members do possess a commitment to the area and each other. There is no insistence on squeezing out every day of holiday entitlement. No complaints about working evenings or weekends. In nearly eight years, not one member has wanted to leave.

TAKING THE KNOCKS

So far, I fear the account sounds like a Mills and Boon novel with a peaceful team running successful services for a contented community. The impression arises from the attempt to give clarity and coherence to what often feels like chaos. To put the record straight, something must be said about failures, criticisms and dilemmas.

The project has failed to cope with some aggressive youngsters and needy adults. Paradoxically, I reckon the very closeness and togetherness which attracts some individuals actually repels others. One alcoholic man will walk out of the centre if it becomes crowded. Occasionally, residents reject us directly. A sixteen-year-old bluntly informed me that I must be the worst social worker in the world after I failed to help him with a serious problem. Recently, the team failed to make sufficient headway with statutory authorities. The result was a boy removed from home because of a school attendance problem. Nor do the groups always display a sense of unity. One outing culminated in a public fight between two young mothers.

Living in the neighbourhood, the project worker is constantly aware of failures. Likewise, there is no escape from community criticisms. Sometimes parents complain that leaders show favouritism towards other peoples' children. One established set of mothers temporarily withdrew when their families did not sign up in time for the Christmas parties and newer arrivals had got in first. Older folk sometimes complain that insufficient control is exercised over the younger elements. Recently, the older teenagers objected that they did not gain sufficient use of the building.

Outside of the community, another source of criticism is that the project is not professional enough. The use of time and petrol to transport people to hospital has been regarded as inappropriate for a trained social worker. The taking of a lone father's child to school each day (while he looks after three others) has been deemed to make him too dependent on the project. To use the jargon, the project workers have neglected to set boundaries and to distance themselves from their clients.

Dilemmas, in which the project workers don't know how to react, are another form of tension. For instance, a teenager admits he is conning the school by getting his mark and then slipping out. The team member, who is trying to win the boy's confidence, has to decide whether to inform the school or parents, whether to take him back to school or whether to let him stay at the centre. To give another example, a terrified wife and child sought shelter at my home from the husband. Apart from being scared of the violent husband, I faced the choice of advising the woman to take steps which might break up the marriage or to persevere with it at the risk of danger to herself.

This description of failures, criticisms and dilemmas is given partly to illustrate the knocks that have to be taken and partly because of the bearing they have on the Christian orientation of the project. Some may actually be the result of the orientation. The Christian concept of servanthood led to the willingness to offer ordinary, practical services to the community which in turn led to the criticism of not being professional. Again, the Christian viewpoint sometimes sharpens the dilemmas. For instance, in regard to the woman seeking shelter, I wanted to uphold the value which Christians place on marriage, yet I also felt she might be safer and happier to leave her husband.

Further, in the face of criticisms, the team wanted to develop a Christian response. A natural reaction was to be self-justifying – 'After all the sacrifices we made for the project, what right have you to tear us to pieces?' Instead, albeit imperfectly, the members want to respond rationally, to evaluate criticisms seriously, and, even when angry, still to regard the critics with respect and love.

Not least, the Christian experience provides some means of coping with the above tensions. Jesus too faced dilemmas. When Jesus faced a woman accused of adultery, he somehow combined an acceptance of the woman while still upholding God's values on marriage. There is an example here for the project workers to follow when torn in different directions. Some of the project workers have close ties with other Christians who attend a small chapel. A little time ago a simple service led by a local dad then blossomed into a close fellowship of believers. They tend to back the project and their love and concern becomes means of encouragement when the going is rough. The support is not confined to this group. After an outing, a nine-year-old boy was run over outside our centre and suffered a fractured skull. For a while his life hung in the balance. Christians from all over the district offered prayers which, in my subjective experience, seemed to encircle us all.

Even with such support, occasionally I feel almost overwhelmed by a sense of failure or helplessness. The experience of 'burn out' is known to many social workers and no doubt non-Christians discover means of surviving. But my – and other members' – means is to turn to God, to find forgiveness for failures and rest and renewal for our exhausted bodies and spirits.

COLLECTIVE ACTION

Clearly, Christian values underpin the services to individuals and groups within the confines of the project. At times, efforts extend beyond these boundaries.

The council estates surrounding the project centre possess none of the gross deprivations of the inner ring of large cities. Yet in common with other working-class areas, they bear the brunt of unemployment, low incomes and lack of facilities. The estates are on the outer fringe of a city whose major investment is in promoting tourism and preserving buildings in the city centre. Thus, the area is vulnerable to decisions which further disadvantage it. To give three examples – there has been a policy of infilling whereby further council houses are built on the remaining play space; the closure of the only post office; and the possible axeing of the comprehensive school.

Should Christians get involved in collective action to oppose such changes? If their identification is with the oppressed, then the answer is 'yes'. The project has allowed its building to be used for meetings while, as a resident, I have joined in the lobbying, campaigns and protests. The score so far is that the post office was closed, the infilling was stopped, the school issue is still open.

Far from steering clear, Christians have a contribution to make to collective action. Jesus was prepared to oppose the religious, civil and military authorities of his day. But he never resorted to slander, misrepresentation or violence. He always bore love towards his enemies. Here again is the example for Christians drawn into movements in Southdown or anywhere else.

CHRISTIAN EXPRESSION

The Christian basis of the project is reflected in its objectives, approaches and attitudes. Is the faith ever expressed more explicitly? One of the boys' junior clubs holds a session on Sunday mornings when quizzes, serials and talks focus on Jesus Christ. A 'Good News' summer play-scheme also has a Christian theme. Three of the team attend the chapel and frequently youngsters drop in to my home for 'a cuppa' before accompanying us there. Of late, Dave Wiles and Jim Davis have found teenagers wanting to gather to question the claims of Christianity. In all these expressions, care is taken that an interest in Christianity is not regarded as a condition for enjoying the project. The boys' club and Good News Scheme are matched by another club and play week which have no religious content. Interestingly, all are fully supported.

The project is known in the community as being Christian. Jesus Christ came to reveal what kind of society we should attempt to build. He also came as a light to dispel the darkness in individual lives. Christians can help to spread that light in the community. The dramatic changes in Dave Wiles' life is still talked about. Consequently, some people feel free to initiate discussion. Occasionally, they arise at times of personal crisis – 'Why did God let my child die?'; 'Why should I get cancer?' Sometimes we try to bring a Christian mind to a debate about unemployment or nuclear weapons. Recently one dad began questioning me about my beliefs and my attitude to the Bible.

CONTINUING APPLICATION

The Christian faith has constituted a source from which the project members have clarified the concepts and principles on which to base their practice. But the clarification is not a static process. Of late, the team has begun to question whether the philosophy of contemporary social work management – with its emphasis on status, prestige, authority and the resulting distancing from the people it is supposed to serve – is compatible with Christian servanthood and humility. Likewise, the team is asking whether differences in income between members are justified. What should Christians do with their own possessions in the light of New Testament teaching? Puzzling as the questions are, the team are convinced the answers can be found in the life of Jesus Christ.

CONCLUSION

Standing outside our centre, a passing mother called to me 'Hey, my son says he believes in God now.' The boy's aggression and stealing had led the mother and step-father to approach me. We had talked about his need for contact with his real father. Warning that I had no magical answers, I invited him into our clubs. Although not gifted at sport, he played football, came swimming and began chatting. He became a regular at our Sunday group. Hence the shouted observation about his belief. Whether due to these influences or not, whether it will continue or not, he has improved. Anyway, the parents are pleased.

Perhaps this small example sums up what community social workers in a Christian agency are trying to do. They desire to be available to people in the neighbourhood; to run clubs and activities which residents want and enjoy; to get close to people who want to talk; to draw upon Christian principles and experience in running a project which both helps and is backed by the community.

CHAPTER 7

Residential Social Work

Keith White

Probably no aspect of social work has been so shaped and influenced by Christian traditions and personnel as residential care. Centuries before social work arrived on the scene in any organized and formal sense, Christian groups were experimenting with residential living outside the nuclear and extended families. In many subtle ways a monastic model has underpinned the ethos and structure of establishments like hospitals, boarding schools and places caring for deprived children and others in need. More obviously the place of formal Christian teaching and worship in residential establishments for children was undisputed from the eighteenth century until the mid-twentieth century.[1]

One of the other major factors shaping British residential care has been the Poor Law. It is impossible to understand modern social work attitudes without recognizing that much present policy and practice is a reaction against Poor Law institutions. Voluntary child care organizations, many of them explicitly Christian in origin, were often started against the backcloth of, and as an alternative to, the Poor Law, and more recently, old people's homes have sometimes been adapted workhouses.

At the present time Christian residential care seems to be running in two rather separate streams. In the one are a vast range of communities seeking to work out, in daily communal living, aspects of the Christian faith that are at variance with the assumptions of the rest of society (chastity, poverty and obedience, for example); in the other are those organizations working in close partnership with the 'formal' social work sector and which tend to operate within categories determined by client-group, lifestage or method of work. Although both streams can be traced back to a common source, they have for so long gone their separate ways that they are usually assumed to flow from separate springs. Throughout this chapter, the first is termed the 'communal' stream; the second, the 'social work' stream.

This false and artificial division between different types of residential experience has had deep effects on the practice of those Christian organizations closest to formal social work. They have tended to accommodate themselves to, and be shaped by, social work models and categories, at the expense of the Christian faith. A glance in one or two of the libraries of major Christian organizations makes the point very clearly: the Christian section is usually the Cinderella of the whole operation. We have not only not thought through residential care 'Christianly'[2] but we have also found ourselves operating within structures and policies that have often been accepted unquestioningly, rarely, if ever, having been examined under the searchlight of the Christian faith and traditions.

For this reason this chapter is not confined to the 'social work' stream of residential care, although that is its focus. In seeking to develop relevant and radical Christian insights it has been necessary to consider not only Christian teaching, but also Christian experience throughout centuries of experiments and traditions. Much of what follows is an attempt to divert or ship water from the first stream into the second! This is a timely exercise for three reasons. First, Christian organizations providing residential care arc now actively tackling the question of what it means to be a Christian organization and how this affects policy and practice. Second, the whole nature of residential care as it relates to social work is being questioned and opened up now as never before. Increasingly specialist provision is being set in a wider context in order to assess its place in the overall scheme of things and to evaluate its effectiveness.[3] Third, since the Second World War there has been a mushrooming of Christian communities of every sort as Andrew Lockley's book, *Christian Communes*[4] and the membership list of the National Centre for Christian Communities and Networks, testify.

There was a time when residential child care was run as, and assumed to be, a separate entity from, say, care for the elderly or mentally ill. Now it is recognized that there are common strands to the residential experience. Therefore this chapter has drawn as widely as possible from different types of Christian communal living, from St Christopher's Hospice to the Laurentius-konvent; from Little Gidding to the Falconer Home in Zambia; from Father Flanagan's Boys' Town to therapeutic communities of the Richmond Fellowship; from l'Arche to Corrymeela. Bearing the wealth of experience of such an immense variety of communities in mind, there are two questions that underlie this exploration: Are there any distinctively Christian insights into the nature of residential care? and What practical impact might a Christian contribution have?

There is no assumption that a Christian perspective is the only one possible, nor that it is normative for every detail of every situation, nor that it is necessarily the best. Often people have arrived at similar conclusions by other very different routes. When mentioning Mill Grove, the place which forms my base of life and work, I do not want to imply that we have found answers to the questions posed in any final sense, but simply that we are seeking to grapple with these questions in a practical way.

SOME CHRISTIAN INSIGHTS INTO RESIDENTIAL SOCIAL WORK

Marriage and the family

By any definition the family is a key unit in social work policy and practice. It is arguable that a simple rule of thumb for social workers is to keep people together and out of 'care' whenever possible. Alternative residential settings and experiences are thus seen as inferior to 'the experience of a family home'. The current upsurge in the popularity of fostering in Britain (though clearly related both to economic considerations, and organizational problems of residential alternatives) would not have been possible were the family not seen as the best group in which to live.

At first sight it might be assumed that a Christian perspective would endorse this view completely. Paradoxically, it offers a radical critique of the modern family. The Bible is specific only about the basics of family living. There is a central place for the life-long covenant of marriage, the command that children should 'honour father and mother' and the duty placed on parents to bring up children to love God. Yet beyond this there is no detailed blueprint for family living. What is more, several aspects of the teaching of the New Testament are a challenge to normal Western assumptions about the family. There is the respect for single people who do not get married; there is the challenge to put God's Kingdom before family; and there are interpretations of family (the worldwide family that prays 'Our Father', and the family of the local church) which open up the nature of family living way beyond the boundaries of the nuclear family.

As we have noted already, the history of the church abounds with examples of community living which are alternatives to 'normal' family life. It is important to note that this is true in Orthodox, Roman Catholic and Protestant traditions, for this trend is not just a particular emphasis of one denomination; it seems to stem from the nature of the Christian faith. Not only have recent decades seen new communities developed which have captured the imagination of thousands (for example, Taizè), but there have also been stringent Christian criticisms of the Western nuclear family.[5] Whereas social work for the most part seems to have overlooked some of the structural problems of the family posed by R.D. Laing and D. Cooper, Christians have not always been so starry-eyed. This is not to suggest that the family is seen as anything but precious and God-given by Christians, but it is to state that the biblical norms for the family are centred on relationships and bonding, rather than on place, a private sphere separated from neighbours, and the consumer-oriented nature of family living.

From the time Hannah offered Samuel to God by taking him to the temple to live, many people in the Christian/Judaeo traditions have shown a preference for alternatives to ordinary family living. It is significant that people today who have the means to choose residential arrangements, often show a preference for alternatives to the family at least for limited periods of time. (For example, boarding schools, private nursing homes, hotels, as well as Christian communities.) Could it be that alternative communities may, in the long run, not only help individual 'clients' but also contribute to the more healthy development of ordinary families by questioning the tyranny of the current Western nuclear family model?

Community

Residential social work is, by its very nature, about 'community'. If it proceeds in ignorance of this fact or seeks to be something different, it will inevitably tend at best towards some sort of treatment-centred approach, where individuals are helped in a way not dissimilar to the model of the health service hospital. At worst it will tend towards a 'warehousing' or 'hotel' model. The family is one sort of community, the local neighbourhood another, the church another. Yet each has become so associated with a set of living arrangements, a geographical area and a building, that it is hard to draw together the common threads by thinking flexibly and laterally. It is a commonplace in social work that we simply do not know enough about 'community' for it to be a useful concept. There are indeed many sources of insights into community, including diverse historical examples from across the world, sociological studies, and organizational experience, but for the purpose of this chapter we shall be looking at the insights afforded by the Christian tradition.

The concept of the Trinity – one God in three persons – difficult though it is to understand, surely indicates that loving relationships are at the heart of the universe. Throughout the Bible there are images of community – flock, kingdom, people, family, household, city. Both Old and New Testaments are concerned not just with individual salvation, but with the creation of new relationships and communities modelled on, and enabled by, the love of God for his creation.

Let me refer to two or three works that have been of particular help to me. Martin Buber's *I and Thou*[6] is one of the most seminal books on relationships and community. In passing, he seems to have found a term that describes many of the places we have created in the name of residential care. He terms them 'It-worlds'. Bonhoeffer's *Life Together*[7] is another classic, and the first chapter with its definition of 'community' centred on Christ is particularly relevant. Andrew Lockley's *Christian Communes*[8] is a helpful source book. The insights of these writers revolve around the notion that community transcends particular locations or living arrangements. It can be destroyed or undermined by bad planning or architecture, or by inappropriate organizational structures, but it cannot be created by or through them. The relationships which are the *sine qua non* of community must be given time and space to grow. In Christian terminology, community (or 'fellowship') is God's gift; it is the work of His Spirit. John Taylor in *The Go-Between God*[9] develops this theme beautifully.

Rarely has social work been able to afford the time or the space to allow real communities to grow. Instead it has attempted 'purpose-built units', 'care and treatment in a planned environment', always seeking to pin down the precise objectives of a place, and to define the method of work. A Christian perspective is timely and appropriate as a counter-balance to this conscious planning and attempted quantification.

The nature of man

(I am, of course, using the term 'man' to mean people, irrespective of gender.) In a recent book, David Lyon has argued that an understanding of the human image portrayed in the Bible can make a significant contribution to sociological theory, knowledge and practice.[10] Any enterprise involving the care, or intended transformation, of people demands, among other things, a view of man. Clearly a view of human nature is needed in the whole of social work

(though there seem at present to be several mutually exclusive con-
tenders, including behaviourism, Freudian and post-Freudian psychoanalysis and Marxism); but it is the immediacy, the totality and
the control of the residential situation that make a declared view so
much more urgent. If a child is being cared for in an establishment,
that child's views of the purpose of life, of the nature of relationships, sexual and other, of the place of work in life, of priorities and
values, will be shaped by the view of man that the carers hold.

One contribution to thinking in this area was the *Barclay Report
1982*, which listed certain of the basic objectives of residential
care.[11] These can all be traced back to Christian roots, and although
they do not make up a Christian view of humankind, they are at
least consistent with it. (The glosses are mine.) The basic needs of
people in residential settings that should be met are given as:

- *A secure base of satisfying and enjoyable experience.* The Garden
of Eden signifies this base in the Bible. So too do the New
Jerusalem and the Kingdom of God. In biblical terms man is
created for an everlasting relationship with the living God.
Without such a secure base, he will always be insecure and restless.

- *Experiences which reinforce each individual's feeling that he
matters.* The centre of the Gospel is that every person matters
deeply to God. It is not possible for a person to know the fullness of
life without the reinforcement from experience that he is accepted
and loved.

- *Relationships with care-givers that are both warmly human and
skilfully adapted to the circumstances of individuals.* The community
that Christ founded broke completely new ground in its mutual care
for all types of people. The epistles of the New Testament abound
with insights into the richness of inter-personal relationships in
Christ.[12]

- *Boundaries which reflect the limits there are to self-expression
and the right of others to respect and choice.* In biblical terms man is
'fallen'; in his original nature he needed boundaries (the forbidden
tree, the limits of the garden), so how much more are such moral
boundaries necessary after the Fall? In the Bible people's 'rights'
are inextricably bound up with responsibilities. Without repentance there can be no forgiveness and without forgiveness no truly
human relationships. (The current trend towards better working
conditions for staff and more 'rights' for clients, exposes the

shallowness of contemporary understanding of the integration of rights and responsibilities in any relationship or community.)

● *Opportunities for friendships outside and within the establishment.* The biblical opposition to self-contained inward-looking groups of people has already been noted in this chapter in relation to the family. Man's social nature will not be fully developed or explored in a single group or a single relationship. He needs both *gemeinschaft* (the close and binding relationships typical of nuclear families and pre-industrial villages) and *gesellschaft* (associations and relationships developed in bigger, and changing, social groups).

● *Opportunities to be creative and to maintain or develop skills... sufficient choices and challenges to equip people for the demands of living independently.* The Bible tells us that God made man in 'his own image', and although every aspect of human nature noted here is some sort of insight into the nature of God, perhaps this desire to create, and explore is as close to the Genesis association of this phrase as any other. The New Testament is full of exhortations to use every God-given talent to the full.

● *The opportunity to explore and learn from the consequences of new experiences.* Given a secure base (ultimately to be found in God alone), the purpose God has for us is to do with exploration of creation. The interaction with creation will be direct and immediate, sometimes very painful. We are not designed to be sheltered from every storm.[13]

This list from the Barclay report is sufficiently full and congruent with the biblical view to be of great practical use to those working in residential care. Every establishment will tend to stress the meeting of certain of these needs rather than others. Thus to have such a range of needs set down serves a corrective function. Taken together, the various aspects of human nature tend to add up to the longing for love and need to love and be loved. If so, and if residential care can be oriented to recognize and, as far as possible, to meet these needs, then this is a notable Christian contribution to the field.

Base for evaluating objectives, methods and interpretations

One of the major problems in residential social work over the past two decades has been the rapid rise and fall of a number of very varied fashions. Units have been opened for one purpose, have been used for something else, and then have been closed. Organizations have espoused quite antithetical causes in close succession, or sometimes at one and the same time. But one obvious reason is the lack of a base from which to analyze, and a gauge against which to judge, any proffered new method of work.

The rival bases for assessing residential care are limited. One is the Marxist framework which is notoriously wooden in assessing many aspects of personal relationships. An alternative is systems theory, which lacks a philosophical foundation. Another base is cost benefit analysis. It seems to me that a Christian perspective brings both a sufficiently coherent view of humankind, and experience and theology of communal living to residential social work which enables a meaningful assessment of certain aspects of methods and objectives. At the same time, it does not tie itself to a particular approach.[14] To illustrate the relevance to present-day social work, let us look briefly at four current approaches to residential social work.

● *The hospital model* relies heavily on the notion of diagnosis and treatment. It assumes two clear groups – those in need and those who treat them. Whereas in a community they must share together in ways that cross this boundary, this model assumes that a person's condition can be accurately diagnosed and treated, at a time when doubt is being thrown on the process of assessment from all quarters. It is also mechanistic in assuming that a given treatment plan will provide the same effects in different people.

● *Behaviour modification* is another approach operating widely at present. Doreen Elliott (herself a Christian) has challenged the approach on several grounds[15] and I have attempted to do so elsewhere.[16] To summarize briefly, deep and lasting relationships, preparation for 'independent' living, the spontaneity of communal living are all under-represented in this system.

● The *'permanency' principle* has come to occupy a central place in certain areas of British child care. It is based on a recognition of the child's need for security, but underestimates the bonding between mother and child over time (and throughout periods of separation), and has a largely uncritical view of the nuclear family.

● *Therapeutic communities* (which see group living and group processes being in themselves potentially beneficial to the emotional health of individual members) have much more in common with a Christian perspective than the other three approaches mentioned, yet if applied uncritically can be wholly inappropriate for children, and can underestimate norms other than those a given group may decide on democratically (e.g. the Ten Commandments).

These comments are brief to the point of caricature, and a much more detailed analysis underlies them. It should be stressed that there may be points of validity in each of these models, and that most families and residential comunities will find themselves adopting one or another of the methods from time to time. Yet these approaches are not adequate in themselves as a basis for residential care or a child care policy, and a Christian perspective provides a useful baseline for evaluating a variety of models.

There will never be an answer to the question of what a Christian model would look like in practice, only a wealth of practical examples of communities which have sought to follow Christ's teaching and example. One of the deep paradoxes of the faith is that Christ demands such total allegiance and obedience and yet this leads to such freedom of experience and action. Christians in residential work will be ready and willing to learn from any insight that others may bring from whatever perspective it comes, provided it is consonant with a Christian view of man as an individual and in community.[17]

Tension between bureaucracy and fellowship

The Barclay Report's conclusions about the conflict between bureaucratic organization and communal living[18] are nothing new. While present in any organization to some degree, the full force of the struggle has probably never been so acute for so many centuries as in the church. At one extreme there has been the attempt to live out in a small community the Christian faith in all its purity, while at the other the church in the middle ages was effectively running one of the biggest organizations of all time. The sociology of religion is replete with studies of this tension. Tight-knit residential communities do not fit neatly into any organizational structure. (The history of the family is a fine example of this.)

In the light of this experience how ingenuous the Seebohm Report[19] of 1968 sounds when it declares that there are no grounds to the fears that a unified social service department would be too big for humanity ... and lose the personal touch. Christian experience and theology (particularly the theology of the Holy Spirit) indicate that you cannot organize community beyond a certain point. You can sow seeds, but these must then be allowed to grow. If you desire small, spontaneous, caring communities then this will have radical organizational implications. Put another way, you cannot modify residential care independently of its structural setting.

This may seem like an unimportant or even tangential insight, but it is of great importance at present. Broadly speaking, the social work stream of Christian organizations has tried to work from the top down, with structures that are not dissimilar to their statutory counterparts; the communal stream has always worked from the small group of committed people outwards. It has eschewed bureaucracies at every stage and turn. It may be that organizational structures have been one of the features that have acted like land-masses keeping the two streams apart. If so, dismantling or restructuring the large organizations, Christian and other, will be no easy matter. Perhaps the most effective and practical response is to begin working in a fully conscious way outside them.

The five areas discussed above do not add up to a coherent Christian perspective or model for residential social work; they are neither comprehensive, nor worked out in detail. Yet they do provide certain Christian bearings, which may prove useful to people involved in this area but who are not committed to the Christian faith.

Having explored insights which have some radical implications for policy, organization and practice, we now turn to a concrete example of a community which is trying to work out the implications of the Christian faith in practice. It started life over eighty years ago as a children's home and would normally be expected to be located within the 'social work' stream. However in learning from experience and from attempts to apply biblical truths in daily living it has increasingly drawn on the other 'communal' stream. Because it is unique in certain respects it may be impossible to reproduce its particular characteristics elsewhere. This should not be a cause for concern as the assumption behind this chapter is that there is no one universal and correct Christian method of care. It is for each person and organization to work out how the faith is translated from 'word' to flesh in different contexts.

THE IMPACT OF THE CHRISTIAN FAITH IN PRACTICE

Mill Grove was founded in 1899 to care for motherless children east of London. The story of its development is fully told in *A place for Us*.[20] It is sufficient for the purposes of this chapter to highlight some of its most important characteristics. It has remained a single community since its inception, and apart from a break during the second World War, has been based in the same building throughout this period. A single family over three generations has been at its heart. At present the residential community numbers about thirty, but well over one thousand people have spent a period of their lives at Mill Grove. There is now a worldwide family network centred on the community, held together by informal links. The community is independent of any larger organization, and though inspired by the Christian faith, is not attached to any one denomination.

The 'children' at present at Mill Grove are all making it their long-term base, but all except three (orphans) have regular contact with their biological families and these families are very much involved in the life of the community. In the normal course of events, children go to nearby day-schools and take as full a part as possible in the life of the neighbourhood. There is no leaving age, and so it is not uncommon to have a very blurred line between 'children' and 'adults' in the community. This is the setting in which the following six practical aspects of the Christian faith have been at work.

Committed Carers

The life and work of Mill Grove would be impossible without committed adults at the heart of the community. This is true of any lasting residential community that is going to grow and develop, including the family. All the carers at Mill Grove are Christians and it is ultimately in response to the love of Christ that they have joined the community. The self-giving love of Christ himself has been the primary motivating force in the church throughout the centuries. There have always been those prepared to give and not to count the cost, to labour and not to ask for any reward save that of knowing that they do his will. Such motivation is in sharp contrast to the attitudes most have towards 'work' in modern western societies, where financial reward and career-development figure most often at the top of a person's priority list.

It is not by chance that communities of the past were built on strong vows and obedience, for without that commitment there is no rock on which the community of relationships can be built, no bone-structure to support the communal body. Increasingly, residential social work has been caught up in 'industrial' disputes.

The intractable problems are becoming obvious to all concerned with this field, and in retracing the history of residential care, the importance of committed carers is being rediscovered. The Barclay Report for example, talked of the need for 'a tenacity of caring commitment to particular individual children, that counts no clock and is not destroyed by rejection'.[21] Without this commitment, not only is there a failure to meet some of the most basic needs of individual residents; but the possibility of real community living is also ruled out.

In the social work stream it is now common to have units where no staff are fully resident and where a detailed analysis of meals and sleeping-in forms part of pay negotiations. In reality, communal living cannot be broken down like this and, indeed, no community can survive people who insist on all their own rights. Inevitably working conditions tend to shift to favour the interests of the paid employees at the expense of clients.[22] Wolins and Wozner specifically mention the significance of staff's living-in in a residential community: 'Staff's residence among the inmates represents their total availability .... their surrender of options implies their commitment to residents.'[23] They conclude that a successful unit will need 'nearly continuous, self-denying behaviour'. They quote approvingly the example of Korczak. When Nazis took the children for whom he cared from the Warsaw ghetto to the Treblinka extermination camp, he remained with them to calm them and eventually to die with them.

There are, of course, dangers in all this. There may be unconscious factors at work which disguise the nature of the carer's motivation; there is the risk of exploitation; there is the risk that the needs of the carers will be unmet or even unrecognized. But the Christian is exhorted to deny himself that he may live. It is an act of faith. In a genuinely caring community, every person, whatever his or her label, is important to the well-being of the whole. The demands of living with 'continuous front-stage exposure'[25] are very great. Yet always when people leave, they feel they have gained by the experience, that in some way they have become more whole.

Deep commitment changes the whole dynamics of the community. Sadly, when clients have been calling loudly and continuously for people 'unconditionally committed to them' (to quote Barclay) they have often been offered poor substitutes. Christians are not better than other people – others will draw an altruistic motivation from different sources – but we have found in practice over eight decades at Mill Grove, many willing helpers who have come in response to Christ's love.

A common cause

Each day at Mill Grove begins with a few adults praying together. They are committed to the same Lord. Formally and informally this common faith permeates the life of the community. In that there are no appeals for funding, food, clothing or personnel except to God in prayer, it would be inappropriate and irrational for adult non-believers to become part of the community. A common cause of some sort is essential to the survival and growth of a community. Wolins in his cross-cultural research, found this to be one of the most vital elements of successful group care. The common cause may vary. Sometimes it will be the specific nature of the task; sometimes it will be the implementation of a method of treatment like behaviour modification. Often, however, there is no deep agreement about the underlying values that unite a community or unit, and this has been an aspect of the social work stream that has been rather neglected by management and organizations. You can perform many tasks (assembling a car, for example) without complete agreement among a team, but the more difficult and testing, the more personal and demanding the task, the more important it becomes to have unity at a deep level. Life in residential communities is exceptionally stressful and testing and there is no short cut or easy way to team spirit and unity.

Without decrying other bases for a common cause, we can at least say that at Mill Grove we have found our unity in Christ to be a stabilizing and yet liberating experience. Diverse personalities, different backgrounds, a variety of interests and experience, all go into the making of the community. It is not simply theology (in the western sense) that unites, but a shared experience of the risen Christ, and a desire to obey his commands and to love one another as he has loved us. We find in him, not a rigid framework for living (like a behaviour modification programme) nor a mechanistic method of working, but a basis for sharing and exploration.

Use of a variety of methods and insights

It has been argued above that some approaches to care do not seem to be consistent with the Christian view of man; it is also true that there are other traditions which illuminate and inform our practice. While most Christians cannot go all the way with Freud or Jung for example, they have undoubtedly helped our understanding of the nature and place of the unconscious in a person's experience.

Likewise, the careful assessment and planning of behaviourists may well provide a way of approaching particular behaviour problems.

In practice at Mill Grove we have used people versed in, and concepts related to, Freudian and Jungian psychotherapy, the writings of Frankl and Fromm, family therapy, groupwork, Bernstein's work on language structures, and so on, as well as drawing widely from Christian sources and experience. Our harvesting of ideas goes way beyond any definable field of social work. The framework for our patterns of living is in itself responsive to the seasons, to local traditions and culture, to rhythms of daily life, to Christian festivals, to life stages.

A mixed community

Residential care in the social work stream has tended to work with selected or categorized groups of people (children, the elderly, those with handicaps). Yet while specialized groups are accepted for limited purposes (for example, in hospital wards or schools), there is something immediately unnatural about groups which form a base for life which label people according to a common problem. Andrew Lockley puts it like this: 'It cannot be very healthy to cram together people, all of whom are categorised as having the same problems, in one group in one building.'[26] In contrast, community is most likely to develop where there is a mixed group of people, in terms of age, sex, talents, handicaps and personality. There is a complementarity of gifts and needs between the elderly and children for example, which is usually recognized in the grandparent-grandchild relationship.

Mill Grove started as a typical voluntary children's home, largely cut off from the surrounding community, with a clear demarcation between staff and children, and an assumed leaving age. Over the decades, all of these boundaries and markers have been blurred. It is no longer a children's home, much more like a rather rambling extended foster-family. Several retired people have chosen to live at Mill Grove; older members of the family often return to stay for varying periods; there is no leaving age; and the links between the Mill Grove community and the surrounding neighbourhood ensure that there is much real communication between people of different ages and type.

In terms of the children who come, we deliberately seek to allow a mixed community to develop. There are boys and girls, of different races, of different intellect and with very different levels of maturity. This has not been planned in any direct sense; it has been a quite natural development of the life of Mill Grove. Because of it, we have avoided many of the problems of the peer group pressure so vividly described in Polsky's *Cottage Six*[27] and have also avoided much of the stigmatisation associated with clearly labelled institutions. We have coped with and helped people with severe problems (for example, terminal cancer, personality disorders, deep-seated childhood traumas, and physical and mental handicaps) in a warm and understanding human environment. The reason for this is the fact that healing and personal growth so often occur in such mixed communities.

Once labels are taken off and everyone is respected and treated as a person in his or her own right, understanding, insights, support, comfort, come from the most unlikely sources. I remember recently a child returning from a weekend with friends that in his view had gone disastrously wrong. It was impossible for me to get through in any way, but a girl just three years older spent the whole evening with him and through being with him, listening and showing that she understood, 'worked through' the traumatic experience with him. The incident was all the more precious and instructive to me because it was so spontaneous and un-selfconscious. Elderly folk have spent hours reading to children, and have, in turn, found the children more than willing to use their legs for them.

By its very nature, the family is likely to be a mixed community in terms of age and personality. Perhaps another of the attractions of fostering is that it gets away from the specialized type of establishment. But whether or not this is so, mixed communities, whether families or neighbourhoods, tend to have a lot of staying power and creativity. A group that is not mixed will create its own problems in addition to those that individuals bring to it. An old people's home and a seaside town dominated by the elderly will throw up similar problems. Where a real sense of community is alive, there is no reason why 'membership' should be restricted to a certain type of person. As I write I think of the playgroup which takes place at St Christopher's Hospice among the terminally ill, the Roslin Community which has welcomed people from mental hospitals to live alongside those committed to the brotherhood, and L'Abri in Switzerland where every possible human category seems to be represented. The discovery of the potential of a mixed community has brought much joy to us at Mill Grove, and in practical terms this may be one of the aspects of our life with the most direct implications for the social work stream.

Use of the family as a model of caring

It may seem strange that having questioned the way the modern family operates and is seen, it should then be used as a model at Mill Grove, but a lot hinges on the way we understand the modelling process. The family has so often been 'aped' in residential establishments, which has lead to impracticalities and even deception. But certain characteristics of the family are vital in any community, and it is these which we have tested at Mill Grove. We have already touched on the importance of committed carers, and mixed groups of people. In addition, the family is, typically, a small, flexible institution with a considerable degree of autonomy and yet closely integrated with other societal institutions (for example, education and health systems). It has permeable boundaries and dynamic roles built into it. Though associated with place, it is based on relationships, kinship bonds and loyalty. It has a long time-span underlying all assumptions – time for growing-up, for exploration, for being. In all these ways it forms something of a contrast to establishments in the social work stream.

The modern nuclear family has serious disadvantages as a model for alternative residential communities – it is too privatised, too consumer-oriented, too close-knit in terms of its expectations. But if the three-generational family is used to complement it, there are many elements instructive in the setting-up and running of alternative communities. Families, nuclear and extended, usually provide the setting where people are loved and able to love primarily as people, as persons in their own right. There are few formal regulations and stated objectives, there are no payments and working conditions. If the family as a model is, therefore, impractical in social work establishments, it is still vital as a corrective to accepted patterns of life and organization.

Again and again clients of all ages who have experienced residential care have longed for certain of the basic elements of family life. Warm and loving relationships, spontaneity and trust are just as possible in a residential community as in a family. The myth that any alternative to the family must have 'neutral' qualities is likely to be a self-fulfilling prophecy in the social work stream. Paradoxically, it is the communal stream that finds a most willing response to the family as a model, the stream which has been most critical of modern developments in family living! It has been our experience at Mill Grove that while children living among us have needed specialist help in a number of respects (remedial education, counselling, for example) there has also been a deep longing for the committed caring associated with the family. Alternative communities will never be families in every respect of the word, nor should they attempt to be so, but they can and do provide for many more personal needs than is generally assumed. The Christian link in all this is once again the commitment of the carers. Just as a life-long marriage is the basis of the Christian family; so whole-hearted commitment is necessary in residential communities seeking to meet the deepest needs of children and adults.

Continuity of care

If one of the problems of past institutional care was that children languished in it too long, one of the most pressing problems now is that too few children find a secure base in or through the social work system. Staff changes, breakdowns of fostering, closure of children's homes, patterns of training, working conditions, administrative procedures, and so on, all conspire to convey the message to a child that he or she is on the receiving end of a set of experiences and relationships that have more than a little in common with an evening's entertainment on television. Every programme starts afresh hoping to keep the interest of the viewer, but with its own separate emphasis and objectives. It is just as hard for the client as for the viewer to develop or maintain a sense of identity in the process.

There is only one way to guarantee continuity – that is by deeply committed relationships. Filing systems and organizational safeguards are not only second-best; they do not begin to address the personal needs of clients. We have been astonished at how long, long-term continuity is at Mill Grove. A day or two ago a person who had left Mill Grove in 1922 appeared on the doorstep, and we are also special to the children and even grandchildren of those who have lived with us. Often it is those children who found it hardest to form relationships while with us, who, years later, continue in deepest contact. Crises or happy events occur and the relationships are shown to be alive and well. It all goes far beyond the notion of aftercare or a leaving age, far beyond anything that can be planned or anticipated, and far beyond any conceivable boundary that could be placed around a professional relationship. When a young lady came to stay at Mill Grove recently after seven years away, the effect on other children was marked. Her presence was a reassurance that when they moved on, there would always be a place to come back to. They would not be forgotten. The continuity of yearly festivals and traditions is important in this respect too, as are the continuing links with churches, neighbours, friends and relatives.

Far too often in the social work stream, we have been unable to offer such continuity for a variety of reasons, yet many clients need it more than anything else. If we cannot meet this need, then we must find others who can.

It would have been tempting to present the practical discoveries of life at Mill Grove as if they proceeded naturally from the Christian insights, but this would have given the impression of too tidy a framework and too one-way a flow! The whole experience has been and continues to be one of discovery and exploration. There are daily surprises, situations and events that challenge any conclusions, however tentative, we had made up to a given date. We find ourselves continually challenged in our daily life by our understanding of the Bible, challenged to do things that are hard to live out in our daily experience. So Mill Grove offers no blueprint or success-story, only the reflections of Christians trying to respond in practical terms to Christ's love.

It would have been possible to make direct links between arguments in the first section of this chapter (for example, on marriage and the family) and descriptions in the second (for example, committed carers; the family as a model). For the most part this has not been attempted because it could make the dynamics of a caring community seem too mechanistic. Mill Grove has grown like an oak tree, rather than developed as an organization or a syllogism!

Mill Grove is firmly grounded in the Christian faith. Other residential communities may turn to different soil. Social work will have a contribution to make to residential situations but it does not provide an adequate base, in and of itself, for the creation of living communities. Their origins lie elsewhere, their boundaries extend far beyond the parameters of social work. The detailed work integrating policy and practice, time and place, Christian insights and social work structures has to be done at ground level, and in the context of real life situations. If this article does no more than create an awareness of the existence of two streams and help to remove a little of that which keeps them apart, it will have served a purpose, but it is of course, written with the conviction that the living water of residential living comes ultimately only from God. It is a gift, not something that can be bought or constructed, and that is no easy truth for secular social work to grasp.

Notes

[1] This aspect of residential life has been partially charted in *Residential Child Care Past and Present*, Keith White, Edinburgh University, 1973, unpublished thesis.

[2] This insightful term comes from Harry Blamires in *The Christian Mind*, SPCK, 1963.

[3] An example of this is the wide-ranging study by Martin Wolins and Yochanan Wozner, *Revitalizing Residential Settings*, Josey-Bass, 1982.

[4] Andrew Lockley, *Christian Communes*, SCM, 1976.

[5] See J. A. Walter, *A Long Way from Home*, Paternoster, 1980.

[6] Martin Buber, *I and Thou*, T. and T. Clark, 1970.

[7] Dietrich Bonhoeffer, *Life Together*, SCM, 1954.

[8] See Andrew Lockley, *Christian Communes*.

[9] John V. Taylor, *The Go-Between God*, SCM, 1972.

[10] David Lyon, *Sociology and the Human Image*, Inter-Varsity Press, 1984.

[11] Barclay Committee, *Social Workers: Their Roles and Tasks*, NISW, 1982, 1, para 4:40.

[12] For example, see 1 Corinthians 13.

[13] See W. H. Vanstone, *Love's Endeavour, Love's Expense*, Darton, Longman and Todd, 1977, for some original and deep thinking on this subject.

[14] For a detailed description of how this might be done, see C.S. Evans, *Preserving the Person*, Inter-Varsity Press, 1977.

[15] Best of 'In Residence', *Social Work Today*/Social Care Association, 1983, Vol. 2, pp. 196-7.

[16] For example, *Why Care?*, Social Care Association 1980, p.26 and a review of *Social Learning Practice in Residential Child Care*, *Social Work Today*, 24 November 1981.

[17] I have tried to work this idea out more fully in 'Respect for the person-in-community' in *Why Care?*, Social Care Association, 1980.

[18] Barclay Committee (see note 11), paras 4.17 and 4.20.

[19] Seebohm Report, HMSO, 1968, para 159.

[20] Keith White, *A Place for Us*, Mill Grove, 2nd Edition 1981.

[21] Barclay Report (see note 11), para 4.57.

[22] See Barclay Report, para 4.20.

[23] See *Revitalizing Residential Settings*, p.192.

[24] As above, p.193.

[25] As above, p.193.

[26] See Andrew Lockley, *Christian Communes*, p.114.

[27] Polsky, *Cottage Six*, Russell Sage Foundation, 1962.

CHAPTER 8

The Field Worker:
The Limits of Love

Chris Hanvey

'And who is my neighbour?'
Parable of the Good Samaritan

The long, seventeen-mile descent from Jerusalem to Jericho was notorious for robbers. Plenty of opportunity here to be attacked, stripped of valuables, wounded and left for dead. It hardly seems appropriate, then, to describe the victim of Jesus' parable as 'lucky' that his plight should have been later seen by three fellow travellers. But, he is rejected in turn, by a priest and a Levite, whose passing by 'on the other side' is a symbol of callous and detached inhumanity.

The first audience of this story might well have expected a third traveller. He could have been an Israelite layman, with a modicum of concern and a willingness to assist the hapless victim. Then the moral would have been complete, with a simple anti-clerical message, providing further grounds for priestly suspicion at Christ's iconoclastic teachings. Instead, the victim is helped back to wholeness by a man who, at that time in Jewish history, would have belonged to the most despised and reviled group in society.

Relationships between Jews and Samaritans could hardly have been worse. Some time within the years AD 6-9, and at midnight, the Samaritans had defiled the Temple at the Feast of the Passover, by strewing dead men's bones onto the floor. It had resulted in irreconcilable hostility, racial segregation and a tension which is sadly all too familiar to twentieth-century understanding.[1] 'Samaritan' was consequently a universal term of scorn and abuse. And yet, here was an outcast, chosen by Jesus in the parable to demonstrate 'love your neighbour as yourself'. This neighbour's humanity and simple actions now seems a paradigm for all that is good in social work practice!

The details in Luke's account are significant. Firstly there was the accurate *assessment* of another man's needs, fuelled by a compassion which prevented him from remaining detached. Then came immediate *action* – oil to soothe and wine to disinfect the wounds. The *caring* is then sustained over night by the Samaritan. Enough

94

money ensures the *continuance of help* and the rescuer only withdraws when a future plan of assistance has been organized. While the priest who walked by rejected one of his own people, this outsider responded selflessly to one of another tribe.

'Who is my neighbour?' would, then, appear to invite a simple response. And yet – in common with so many of Christ's parables – the simplicity also hides a number of equally complicated and profoundly disturbing questions. This chapter attempts to explore just a few of these and their supreme importance for social work.

It is not by chance that the parable uses the word 'compassion'. This is a principal motive for the Samaritan's involvement. While Thomas à Kempis warned us against intellectualizing an emotion, in a parallel example ('I had rather feel compunction than understand the definition of it') we are entitled to struggle a little with the meaning of 'compassion'. With its Latin roots, the word implies suffering *with*, feeling pity *for* and is partly summoned up in Thomas Hardy's invented term, 'fellowfeel'. It invariably involves an imaginative leap from where you are, to where the victim or other person is and – when partly explained as 'empathy' – is enshrined in the basics of social work counselling or casework: 'Empathy means entering into the experience of another person by the human and democratic method of sharing experiences.'[2]

But here is one of the first major icebergs, almost totally submerged beneath the parable's calm surface. No one can keep on indefinitely suffering with or entering into the experience of others; and what happens when the wayside appears to be cluttered with men and women who have fallen amongst real or metaphorical thieves?

Every day busy social work area or district offices are crowded with people who need their wounds binding, soothing and healing. They need plans to be made for their future care and comfort. While they may share common problems, 'Each man is not only himself, he is also the unique, quite special, and in every case the important and remarkable point where the world's phenomena converge, in a certain manner, never again to be repeated.'[3] Thus, the many demand and deserve a response, as if they were the one.

Yet it is difficult for welfare agencies to give continually in this unique and individual way. 'Oil' and 'Wine' may be in short supply and the 'two pieces of silver' are increasingly needed for a whole range of human predicaments. It seems inevitable, then, that two major processes take place: the organization at first seeks to categorize and, later, to bureaucratize.

By categorizing people's individual problems it becomes

possible to place parameters on the extent of involvement. It is a human response to put boundaries around the chaos and to seek limitations for that suffering towards which one feels some personal responsibility. Put facetiously and perhaps unfairly it would invite a fourth response in the parable: 'Sorry, we don't deal with men who fall among thieves, you want the Department of...' By putting people into categories, 'the mentally handicapped', 'the elderly' or 'mentally ill' become homogenous groups, not people, who can then be fitted into certain types of boxes for certain kinds of services. These groups in turn invite a similarly stereotyped response from carers, breeding that worse kind of professionalism, attacked by the paralyzed victim of Brian Clark's play:

> 'You and the doctors with your appalling so-called professionalism, which is nothing more than a series of verbal tricks to prevent you relating to your patients as human beings.'[4]

At the same time, systems and organizations are set up and the inevitable bureaucracy is rationalized as the best way of dealing with the many. Caring, as such, can become a very small part of the organization, held together by professional ladders with those who fight for resources or those who distribute them. Perhaps it is an additional sadness that the organization of churches should sometimes seek to imitate these same structures. There is for example a central London Consortium of churches who 'buy into' facilities for destitute men and women and refer such people on to St Martin in the Field's, when assistance in another parish is sought. At one level this is a logical and tidy response to limitless need, at another it may sadly be recognized as the response of a bureaucracy.

Yet, within the constraints of this categorizing and bureacratizing are individuals who try to operate their own sets of values, attempt to see the uniqueness of individual need and seek to recognize, with the late David Wills, that 'the only thing that was likely to create a situation where healing could take place was a situation in which people felt themselves to be loved and felt able to return that love.'[5]

Does the parable fail us, then, because of its inability to grasp the problems of sheer numbers? Is its applicability to daily life, social work or the experiences of an area team, for example, limited or curtailed because we have to face the many and not just the one? It might be argued that numbers are more accurately a challenge of human limitations, of our own boundaries and of our capacity for giving.

From what source, then, does compassion spring? It would be comforting to think that Christianity had a monopoly, but this is not the case. After all, it was not just the agnostic who left the man by the wayside. In the same way, alongside the tradition of great Christian reformers, like Wilberforce, Buxton and Shaftesbury, we find agnostics and atheists of equal courage and vision. This, then, raises the second major issue for social workers.

The Samaritan responded with 'compassion'. Need was relatively easy to estimate and could be met in mainly practical terms. For the field social worker, need may not always be so easily identified and is sometimes only answered through the assumption of many and varied rôles.

In the 1907 Probation and Offenders Act there is an exhortation to probation officers, to 'advise, assist and befriend'. In the last of these rôles the probation officer or social worker most probably parallels the Samaritan. For an elderly person, for example, the woman from 'the welfare' might be the only visitor and link with a world which is perceived as care-less and seen almost exclusively on a TV screen. Subtly, almost imperceptibly, representatives of large departments come to be seen in a different light, as providers – in an unsentimental way – of a friendship which may be difficult to establish with others. But the rôle is a difficult and challenging one. When it is love that is really wanted, friendship may never be enough.

In *Love's Endeavour, Love's Expense*[6], W.H. Vanstone explores some of the complexities of loving, within both a human and a divine context. He draws upon a set of benchmarks for testing the authenticity of love and describes love itself as knowing no boundaries, not seeking to control and all self-giving. Love is thus limitless, precarious and vulnerable. He notes that kindness under its own name may be sufficient but it can become an affront when it masquerades as love or when it is really love that is sought from the other. When love is expected, no kindness, however lavish is sufficient. Such beliefs are found occasionally in social work literature, as they are in Christian theology:

> 'To profess love or to profess to care and then withdraw when that caring impinges on one's own needs or happiness, is only to open wide the wounds, to make them bleed.'[7]

For the social worker, as friend, such a dilemma is ever-present – often faced with limitless needs for love and not able to give it.

The field social worker may also be a provider of resources. These may range from the provision of simple bath aids or disabled car badges, to the allocation of fostering placements, beds in homes or access to hostels and hospitals. All allocation and distribution involves the accurate assessment of another person's needs. There is an element of power within the relationship where one 'side' has the service required by the other, and there is also potential for hurt, disappointment or rejection when these needs are not met. Such giving involves awareness of our own reasons and motives for responding, the inevitably subjective nature of any response, and a consciousness of any variations in our daily or monthly view of priorities and in ways of judging the best method of meeting those needs. In the complicated rôle of giver or provider, the social worker is also closest to his third and perhaps most difficult rôle.

Few would argue that as the representative of a local authority, for example, with certain legislative powers to perform, the social worker is most consistently exercised and challenged. A growing volume of legislation during the last ten years has been accompanied by an increasing awareness of the statutory powers inherent in social work power, in certain circumstances, to remove children from their natural parents; to admit patients compulsorily to psychiatric hospitals or to remove people from their homes. Few social workers feel comfortable with these powers, or would argue that they make the tasks much simpler. Most respond with that degree of anxiety which accompanies a motorist coming across a road-side accident. Sleeves are rolled up and help is given, but with very little confidence that he has been of use, and a hope that he has not done any further damage.

Few elements of the field social worker's many roles has received more publicity in recent years. Pilloried for inactivity or chastened for assuming what are seen as Draconian powers, the social worker often appears incapable of winning. Bewildered parents, thinking they have found a friend, find what they later perceive as an authority prepared to remove their child. This best characterizes one of the many dilemmas which are the daily fare of field social work.

For some practitioners, social work is seen as possessing a further, often unspoken rôle. It is said that we all experience hunger both for bread and for the soul. On occasions a social worker seems to have a responsibility towards the soul, as well as struggling to provide the bread. As a kind of secular priest, his rôle may range from 'acceptance', for behaviour or activities which the bearer is too afraid to admit to others, through to comfort, moral support and, occasionally, relief from guilt.[8]

In my own practice, this hunger has been most vividly experienced in work with mentally ill people. Often the symptoms express themselves in a guilt for some past action, demanding a kind of absolution – diagnosed, more acceptably in twentieth-century society, as 'madness'. 'Mankind,' as T.S. Eliot asserted, 'cannot bear too much reality' and the heavy burden of guilt, carried around by all of us, finds some kind of outlet in varying ways. So often, admissions to a psychiatric hospital have seemed to me not only a logical response to overwhelming guilt and sadness, but also a demand for sanctuary, a cry for absolution and a relief from suffering. Perhaps the label of mental illness is more acceptable to us all?

Lastly, in his perception of human need, the field social worker has a much wider rôle. The prophet Isaiah put it this way:

> 'The kind of fasting I want is this: remove the chains of
> oppression and the yoke of injustice, and let the oppressed go
> free. Share your food with the hungry and open your homes to
> the homeless poor'[9]

and recognized, more mundanely, in both the Barclay Report and in community work literature:

> 'At one level, these problems are very practical, immediate and
> particular to each individual client. What advice does this
> person need? What resources would help her solve her
> problems. Whose responsibility should this be? But at another
> level the problems are much more general, for each of these
> particular cases raises fundamental issues about the sort of
> society we are living in, and the role of social work, and of the
> social services of the 'welfare state.'[10]

It is the rôle of the community activist, the worker who, in Beatrice Webb's terms, assists in the draining of swamps, as well as helping to pull out individual victims. It means working *with* rather than *for* or *on* communities. Furthermore, it involves a true radicalism, shown by churches in some areas of South America, for example. It is firmly located amongst the poor and the oppressed and struggling for the betterment of communities and societies within which individual problems are located.

This list of social work rôles is by no means exhaustive. Yet, it helps to illustrate the rich diversity which exists under the label of field social worker. A logical conclusion might be that trying to combine so many rôles is an impossibility. Often we cannot provide love, although kindness is sometimes possible. We cannot always deliver the necessary resources, although in many cases no amount of resources – if available – would be sufficient to meet the needs of daily practice. We are forced to face the powerful and seemingly punitive roles of executing child care or mental health law, often in the face of public hostility or misunderstanding. We cannot ourselves bring absolution or relief from guilt, although sometimes acceptance of an individual affords some relief from a previously unnamed crime or unspoken burden. And, finally, although we cannot bring an end to the 'dis-ease' of a community, we can work for the alleviation of those wider problems that are put into focus by daily, individual practice.

At the very heart of this activity has to be that compassion which moved the Samaritan to action. Compassion which was linked to the accurate and careful assessment of need and to the provision of those equally necessary resources. Perhaps one of the parable's major lessons for the fieldworker, and one of the main features of Christianity itself, is the challenge to continue responding to the individual, even in the face of the many, with the constraints of the organization itself and against a wider societal ambivalence.

At the end of *The Case Worker* Konrad's anti-hero has been bruised and battered by his social work practice. He is reduced to some degree of passivity, but in sentiments echoing the 'comfortable words' of the Communion Service he offers:

> 'Let all those come who want to: one of us will talk, the other will listen; at least we shall be together.'[11]

At least, like the Samaritan's action, it is a start.

Notes

1 See Joachim Jeremias, *Rediscovering the Parables*, SCM, 1966.
2 Clifford R. Shaw, *The Jack-Roller*, University of Chicago Press, 1930.
3 Hermann Hesse, *Demian*, tr. W.J. Strachan, Peter Owen: Vision Press, 1958.
4 Brian Clark, *Whose Life is it Anyway?*, Amber Lane Press, 1978.
5 David Wills, in *Community Care*, 28 February 1980, p. 22.
6 W. H. Vanstone, *Love's Endeavour, Love's Expense*, Darton, Longman and Todd, 1977.
7 T. Hart, *A Walk with Alan*, Quartet Books, 1973.
8 See Robert Waelder, 'The Scientific Approach to Casework'. *Social Casework*, October 1941.
9 Isaiah 58:6,7.
10 Bill Jordan, *Invitation to Social Work*, Martin Robertson, Oxford, 1984.
11 G. Konrad, *The Case Worker*, Trans P. Aston, Hutchinson, 1975.

PART 3

Ethics and Issues

CHAPTER 9

The Question of Abortion

Lydia Gladwin

An unplanned pregnancy represents a crisis for most of the women with whom we become involved, both in facing the situation and in making a decision. Our personal position, when we are called upon to make a professional contribution to decision-making on the question of abortion, is perhaps one of the most complex we have to reach.

The beginning of my own career coincided with dramatic changes in British law through the implementation of the 1967 Abortion Act. Although we now have a very different framework, a wide range of viewpoints is always likely to be with us. Social workers may find their own personal positions at a variety of points within the total spectrum.

There are two books I would particularly recommend to anyone wishing to examine the various issues from a Christian position. Rex Gardner's book, *Abortion – the Personal Dilemma*, looks at the medical, social and spiritual issues.[1] The author writes as a practising Christian gynaecologist and his consideration is balanced, thoroughly helpful and comprehensive. Oliver O'Donovan, *The Christian and the Unborn Child*, writes from the perspective of a theologian.[2] His approach, alongside Gardner's, enables the reader to understand the nature of responsible Christian opinion on the subject.

It is particularly useful to think both generally and specifically with actual case examples in mind. There is one in my own experience which I would like to relate. Barbara was just sixteen when her first child was born. She had been brought to the United Kingdom from British Guyana by her parents a few years earlier. She left school prematurely and went to live with the father of the child. A second child was conceived within a few months and shortly before his birth, that relationship broke down.

Barbara left hospital to care for her two children alone. Very soon she became involved with a married man by whom she had two more children in quick succession. She referred to him as Mr A and although he did not live with her, he was almost always to be found in the home when I began to work with her at that time. He was from the West Indies and from this cultural background he brought an affectionate and warm relationship with the children, particularly with his own. Yet he seemed irresponsible both in his attitudes to fatherhood and to parental responsibility generally as considered necessary for healthy child development, let alone Barbara's own need to rely on his care and support. Consequently, there were grave concerns about the adequacy for provision for the children's basic needs and indeed for their safety as they were frequently left unattended.

When Barbara found she was expecting her fifth child she seriously considered abortion for the first time. Knowing that her capacity as a parent was already being questioned, it was extremely difficult to be certain of the real issues at stake for her. Quite apart from sheer poverty, inadequate housing, lack of support and personal limitations, the situation was compounded by serious emotional deprivation in Barbara and Mr A, as well as the implications for the existing family of an additional member. Although her behaviour was unreliable, Barbara was hardly mentally unstable in psychiatric terms.

She became quite depressed and anxious as she attempted to resolve the circumstances for herself. She was twenty-three years old, healthy, single and already the mother of four. Her own mother's marriage had failed and she could not look to her for support any more than from the expected child's father. Having sufficiently come to terms with her fear of my potential power in the situation, she discussed in some depth the pros and cons of requesting abortion.

She had had some Christian teaching as a child, and her situation brought to the surface much feeling about her own illegitimacy and considerable guilt about her own lifestyle, which she shared with me. Her expectation that authority figures would hold Christian and judgemental views made the task even more difficult; but a desire to experience the Creator as one who forgives and understands our human frailty was the most positive element in what felt like an almost intractable problem.

I was considerably exercised as to my own perceptions and integrity as well as my professional rôle and responsibility. I supported her in the initial approach to her general practitioner who referred her to a specialist unit. The request for abortion was refused and sterilization offered later and so, almost with a sense of relief, Barbara's fifth child and third girl joined the family.

Eighteen months later the sixth pregnancy was confirmed. Still Barbara refused to consider sterilization and was convinced that an abortion would not be agreed without her consent to the former. The focus of much of my work with her continued to be around the ethical issues of sexual behaviour, birth control and abortion. The sixth baby, which she adamantly claimed would be the last, proved also to be almost the final straw in terms of her maternal skills. The children had to be received into Care for some months and I was exercised as to what the future should and could hold for them.

As might have been predicted, Barbara turned her back on her children for a period and took full advantage of her freedom. Another pregnancy brought the turning-point. It was then that Barbara seemed to face her own vulnerability and responsibility. In lengthy discussion with the medical team, I supported Barbara in her request for termination and sterilization. She suffered emotionally and grieved openly, to a degree I had not anticipated. She wanted to understand more of the purpose of life and matured considerably. She not only kept in regular contact with the children from that time, but also co-operated with efforts to restore them to her care. Once they were home again, I also found it interesting that she sought baptism for them and in so far as her lack of routine allowed, sent them to Sunday School.

This case history seems to raise a full range of questions as we look at abortion. First, *the task of assessment*. In some areas it is not possible for every woman requesting abortion to be offered even one interview with a social worker and some are missed within the group considered most at risk. Mary Burstow and Debra Horowitz Dodd note that 'patients not referred for counselling prior to decision, sometimes present crises as in-patients'.[3] They see the social workers' dual role in counselling and assessment, as being concerned primarily with understanding the woman's request for termination and what the pregnancy represents for her. Second, we are involved in *the decision-making process* and have responsibility for identifying possible contra-indications. In the same article the authors' expressed objective is to 'help the woman reach a constructive solution to her dilemma and to use the experience for maximum learning and growth'. For the Christian social worker this must include recognition of the potential life to be terminated. There are the implications for all the different people involved – the woman, the father, the unborn child and the medical and social work professionals.

When a woman says, 'I cannot bear this child' and considers an abortion the London Diocesan Board for Social Responsibility Working Party concluded 'she is the person most deeply concerned with *making a conscientious decision*'.[4] Respect for her crucial part in the decision is all the more important when the long history of compromise and injustice, which has condemned women to a subordinate and passive role, is acknowledged. The demand made by some for a woman's absolute right to abortion by choice is part of the developing awareness of women's self-determination. The sisterhood of women supporting each other in childbearing and childbirth, understanding the pressures of life and at times helping each other to avoid childbirth, can be a powerful experience. Unless Christians can provide an equally strong experience of affirmative support, the church often has little to offer beside this vital life-line of female friendship.

As part of a family, a wife has the responsibility for sharing her thinking and decision-making with her husband. The single woman certainly has more individual responsibility, but a good decision will take into account many other factors, and as far as possible, involve the father and other significant relatives. At present a putative father has no legal right to any part in any decision about abortion. When he is seeking to act responsibly in the best interests of the woman and the unborn child, then he would seem to have a moral right to take some part in the decision as he did in the conception. The right of the unborn child should not be diminished, and this involves two key questions which Christians concerned to think through the moral issues need to ask.

The first is 'When does individual human life begin?' This question requires the judgement of scientific opinion. Some would say that since all the distinctive features of individual life are present once fertilization is complete, from that point on we are dealing with individual human life. Others would hold that not until individuation is complete – after fourteen days – can we talk of individual life. Up to then, the embryo can split and form twins.

The second question is 'At what point is it right to afford human life the full protection which we are to give to individual persons?' This requires a moral judgement. Here Christians disagree. Some believe that once there is individual life, even if it is still in a very early stage, it has a right to full protection. We are dealing with our own flesh and blood, with all its potentiality for human experience and therefore we have a duty to protect it. Others believe that it is not possible to offer the same protection to life still in the early stages of its potentiality as we do to independent human beings. Until the foetus has the structure of life necessary for normal human experience, it cannot be given equal status with other humans. Human life in its early embryonic stage is only a potential person. It is not until it reaches a stage where it may be seen as a person, that it is to be fully protected. Writers such as Rex Gardner and Oliver O'Donovan will help the reader understand and make their own judgement on this debate.[5]

Our judgement on these questions profoundly influences what we believe is acceptable in practice. The professional person, however, has the added responsibility of being the servant of others while they are forming decisions of their own. It is not always easy to accept that others will decide upon actions which, whilst acceptable in legal and social terms, are outside our own personal moral terms of reference. It is therefore essential that we are clear in our attitude towards this dilemma before we engage in our professional duty.

The law does not permit a termination to be carried out once the child is capable of being born alive, unless it is done to save the mother's life. After twenty-eight weeks of pregnancy the child is presumed to be so capable. But with the constant advancement of medical practice it is possible for a child born at twenty-four weeks of pregnancy (six months) to survive given a strong constitution and the best possible medical care.

OPTIONS

Thus we have considered briefly the external framework and boundaries in which client and social worker begin to explore the options open to her, that is to proceed with the pregnancy, to have an abortion, or to place the child for adoption. The main areas that need to be explored together, with the help of professional insights and experience, will now be considered.

First there are the *circumstances surrounding the conception*. Many conceptions occur with mixed feelings so that not having used adequate contraception may indicate a conscious, or unconscious desire to become pregnant. The explanations given for the unplanned pregnancy might include that it was accidental – that intercourse was unexpected or the contraceptive method used failed; or it may be linked to conflicts about sexuality, for instance, fears that taking the pill may lead to promiscuity. An unwanted pregnancy can result from emotional distress due to events occurring around the time of conception. Loss of any kind, bereavement, or changes in social circumstances such as leaving home, parental separation, birth of a sibling, threatened loss of a partner – all may give some indication of why the pregnancy has occurred at this particular time and what it means to the woman.

Second, it is important to explore *the woman's response* to becoming pregnant, and particularly her initial reaction. What does this expectation of a child and proposed termination really mean to her? Her early feelings may reflect her true response to the discovery and this may change as the father and others learn of the pregnancy. It is vital to learn, through the way in which she talks about the pregnancy, the degree of attachment to the unborn child. For instance, those who refer to the foetus as a baby and wonder about the sex and appearance may be expressing a level of feeling and desire to continue the pregnancy. Others speak in terms of wanting to 'get rid' of the foetus, which they experience almost as some foreign invader.

Assessing the degree of commitment, stability and emotional support within *the relationship with the father* of the child, is a third and crucial area and whenever possible is best done in a joint interview. If the woman is no longer involved with the father, then it is important to explore her feelings about the breakdown of that relationship, which may have reached a turning-point when he learned of the pregnancy. If they are a married couple or have established a relatively stable relationship, then we need to ascertain the impact the birth of the child or an abortion would have on their relationship in the context of their total lives — physical factors, emotional/spiritual capacities, and social circumstances. Here it is important to discuss all the options available, including adoption, so that the best possible decision can be reached on the basis of accurate information and sensitive reflection.

In exploring the *underlying motives* behind the pregnancy, one often senses that the married woman hoped to reinstate a happier period in the marriage by becoming pregnant. Her husband invariably does not respond as anticipated, and out of an already stressful situation arises the request for an abortion. For the single woman, the motive could be attributed to a desire to consolidate the relationship, perhaps even to marry as a result of the pregnancy. In both these situations the request for the abortion reflects the feelings of rejection, anger and hurt towards the father which are displaced on to the unborn child. The father seems to exhibit a cruel, rejecting attitude resulting in the woman wanting to rid herself of his baby. Symbolically she may be trying to free herself of her hurtful and uncomfortable feelings by having an abortion. This is ironic when originally she may have used the pregnancy so that her husband or partner would remain with her and this often results in a double agony of loss.

The taking of a *family history*, its size, the woman's place in it, parental relationships and the quality of parenting will all influence her experience of pregnancy and attitude to abortion. Any diffi-

culties associated with childbearing in her original family, miscar-
riages, still-birth or the death of a sibling may be especially
pertinent. For example, someone whose own mother had difficulty
conceiving her, may feel guilty about seeking a termination. Not
wanting a baby may be associated with feeling unworthy to become
a mother. This often occurs with women who have felt unwanted
by their own mother and the ambivalence towards the unborn child
is a response to their mother's ambivalence towards them.

Understanding what the pregnancy actually represents for the
couple or for the woman on her own is crucial if there is to be any
therapeutic effect of our intervention. One way of achieving this
is to be alert to possible areas of conflict. There is the obvious
conflict between wanting and not wanting a baby, continuing or
terminating the pregnancy. This is often not the main difficulty.
For single girls, having to face parents and others can be a major
obstacle in continuing the pregnancy. The fear of revealing extra-
marital sexual activity and risking rejection can be very real, not
only for young women but also for those brought up in restrictive
families. A small percentage of clients will have deep moral or
religious beliefs which conflict with having an abortion. Their
feelings of guilt and conflict surrounding their situation is an
important area for discussion and in my experience those clients
are particularly appreciative of shared insights of God's purposes
and ethical considerations.

Despite many studies examing the *psychological effects* of abortion, the findings have been varied and indeed conflicting so that it
is still difficult to predict with certainty those women who will be
most likely to be at risk of particular disturbance following a termination. It is important that a woman should not feel the need to
demonstrate some emotional disorder in order to qualify for an
abortion by, for example, threatening suicide. Some women deny
conflict about terminating their pregnancy while others are more in
touch with their mixed feelings.

For most women, having an abortion is likely to be a painful
experience involving a period of mourning for the aborted embryo
and all that the pregnancy represented. Unresolved conflicts or
denial of ambivalence and grief may place a woman at greater risk
following the experience. This may also provoke a woman into
quickly becoming pregnant again when her circumstances may be
unchanged or even less favourable, so it is important to explore the
feelings of guilt and shame following the abortion.

The number of *adolescent girls* seeking abortion in recent decades
has continued to be a cause of concern in our society. The needs of

the girl and her parents would seem to be best met by both separate as well as joint interviews. In this way the parents can be encouraged to express their feelings of rage or grief that their daughter is no longer a child, about her now overt sexuality and recognition that their daughter must make her own decision about terminating her pregnancy. For the young woman it may help her to separate her feelings from those of her parents and to accept responsibility for her behaviour. The normal difficulties associated with abortion are likely to be compounded by immaturity, and parental pressure as well as apathy about the future, poor employment prospects, and attention-seeking characteristics of this age group.

It is salutary for us to realize that in about ten per cent of women who are offered counselling when seeking a termination of pregnancy, there have been one or more previous abortions. As Juliet Cheetham points out,[6] the attitudes of professionals involved with women considering abortion have a considerable influence on the level and nature of the service available.

The complexity of the task is daunting. However, as a Christian and as an experienced professional, I find more difficulty in understanding an absolutist position for social workers on this issue of abortion. It seems to me that there must be a question of the lesser evil in so many situations, and the more as a result of our additional insights and shared responsibility in casework with women making their decisions.

As Professor John Stallworthy reminds us in his challenging forward to Rex Gardner's book, many of us who are deeply concerned by the moral, ethical, religious, physical and mental issues involved in abortion, are constantly searching for facts on which to base our judgement. Though willing to modify formerly held attitudes to this subject, we wish to have assurance that by doing so we are taking action which is justifiable and right.

Notes

1   R.F.R. Gardner, *Abortion – the Personal Dilemma*, Paternoster Press, 1972.
2   Oliver O'Donovan, *The Christian and the Unborn Child*, Revised Edition, Grove Booklets on Ethics, No. 1.
3   Mary Burstow and Debra Horowitz Dodd, 'A Woman's Dilemma', *Social Work Today*, 19 March 1984.
4   London Diocesan Board for Social Responsibility, *Abortion – a Discussion Brief*, 1984.
5   See notes 1 and 2 above.
6   Juliet Cheetham, *Unwanted Pregnancy and Counselling*, Routledge and Kegan Paul, 1977.

CHAPTER 10

Sexuality in Social Work

Julia Staples

'Sexual feelings constitute a potent force to be used to enhance the richness and meaning of life, but by the same token, they constitute a force that can be misused in ways that are damaging to the individuals concerned and to the society of which they form a part.'[1]

What does a social worker do when confronted by distraught parents who claim that one of her colleagues has 'interfered with' their son, or when an adolescent boy, finding her alone, unzips his trousers and starts to masturbate, or comes up to fondle her breasts? When a young male volunteer is insisting that there is nothing wrong with his wish to bathe teenage girls, or when the parents of a mentally-handicapped child are saying that their child does not have sexual feelings, but at the same time asking for help in stopping behaviour which they consider unacceptable? What do I say to the teenage girl I escort to the VD clinic? These are all examples drawn from my own experience of residential social work. They represent the kind of dilemmas which face all social workers.

What response does the social worker make? If the social worker happens to be a Christian, is there a response which is a distinctly Christian 'line'? Is there a set of rules which may be brought to bear in each instance? 'The Bible says ...' But what does the Bible say? These are some of the issues discussed in this chapter.

Let me say at the outset that those who look to this chapter for easy answers to dilemmas similar to the ones which I have presented will soon be disappointed. Search as we will, there is no one set of 'answers' either in the doctrine of our faith, or issued by the people who employ us. There are indeed those who would still maintain that sexual relationships outside of marriage are 'sinful', and some who hold that even within marriage sex is to be tolerated only as a necessary part of procreation, and for whom sex is a taboo subject, seldom to be thought of, let alone spoken about. If ever it is mentioned it is in a negative or condemning way. Those of us brought up with this attitude to sex are left with an inheritance of guilt, shame and sometimes ignorance regarding our own sexuality, which makes it difficult for us to even begin to look at the problems which face other people in their sexual relationships and experiences. We find it such a difficult subject to talk about that we use the trip to the VD clinic to talk about the weather, holidays, or any other subject that will hide our embarrassment.

How shall we begin to resolve some of these questions if there are no set answers? Perhaps we need to look at certain principles which may help us to begin to draw up our own guidelines or frame of reference.

First, Christians believe that men and women are created by God – not as an inventor would 'create' a robot, but with all the complexity of human emotions, thoughts and feelings, and with physical, emotional, intellectual and spiritual needs and drives. To the extent to which we deny any part of our unique personality, we deny one of God's gifts to us. Our sexuality is just as much a part of our humanity as our ability to reason or our capacity to care for others. As with all those parts of ourselves which for some reason may have become detached or repressed, we must first of all accept our sexuality in order that it may truly become a positive force enhancing the richness and meaning of our own lives and those of the people with whom we work.

If sexuality is not sinful and is a gift from God, does that mean that any sexual behaviour is acceptable? This is where our second principle must be brought in. God did not create individuals to live in isolation or in a vacuum, but in relationship to other people. Our relationships must be based on respect both for the worth and integrity of the individual, and for the wider community. All our actions should reflect this. When a person is exploited or coerced into sexual actions against his or her will, then this is unacceptable.

Many people would wish to go further than this and say that any sexual actions which are not the result of mutual decision-making, could be seen as immoral in that they are devaluing to the individuals concerned, and damaging to the relationship. Loving relationships built on trust, respect and mutual sharing can be enhanced by sexual expressions of these feelings only if the feelings and desires are mutual. Constance Lindemann claims that 'a married woman is generally expected to engage in sex with her husband under any conditions.'[2] She argues that social work often contributes to this expectation, a 'good sex life' being seen as the answer to all ills. She goes on to suggest that freedom of choice should include sexual freedom with its many options, including the right to abstain from sexual activity at times.

Sexual relationships cannot be seen simply in terms of the two people directly involved either. As with all close relationships, there will be other people who are either directly or indirectly affected. On the whole, Christians believe that marriage and the family (though not simply the nuclear family) continues to be the best environment in which to bring up children, and sexual relationships should be such that seek to preserve marriage and family life. Michael Rutter[3] argues strongly that morality in this context goes beyond the traditional Christian rules. He says that it is not enough to want to have children, but that children should be wanted for their own sake and not ours, and that there should be a lasting commitment to bring them up in the context of loving relationships.

'Love your neighour as much as you love yourself,' said Jesus. He did not say love your neighbour *instead* of yourself as I suspect many of us in the 'helping' professions interpret this statement, but perhaps what he was saying was something much deeper and far beyond this. What do I really want *most* for myself in my relationships? In the light of this, what do I want for my neighbour? Honest answers to these questions could safely provide a framework for the development of relationships based on an understanding of each other and of the other people whose lives we touch.

CHILD ABUSE

Yesterday a friend, a social worker at a health centre, told me of a five-year-old child who had been brought into surgery with vaginal bleeding caused by some traumatic incident, they know not what. Jessica Hallam writes movingly of her own experiences, '... by the time I was seven I was utterly trapped. With extreme gentleness Daddy would wake me in the middle of the night ... crowded into my little bed. And then would come the guided tour of his body. I was enjoined to silence ...'[4]

These are two obvious examples of sexual behaviour which is exploitation by adults of children, and it seems unnecessary to say that according to any moral standards, this is unacceptable. The question arises, what does one do? As with other forms of child abuse, perhaps the first thing is to attempt to break down the wall of silence which surrounds these occurrences, for only then will the people involved be in a position to receive the help they so much need. This will inevitably involve dealing with our own prejudices first so that through acceptance and understanding of the person we are able to provide a safe structure for the expression of feelings of anger, guilt and so on. Without this help their negative influence will continue to be both powerful and damaging to that person's life. Similar arguments and responses will also apply when we are involved with the victims and offenders in cases of rape.

TEENAGE SEX

Less straightforward is the type of sexual behaviour involving teenagers who are convinced that they are 'in love' and see sexual intercourse as a natural part of this. In adolescence young people are struggling to find their own identity and at the same time puberty brings with it newly-aroused sexual feelings which tend to be all-encompassing. Physical sexuality reaches maturity long before emotional and social development is complete. Since sexual feelings develop in relation to sexual experiences and most adolescents fall in and out of love many times, sexual behaviour begun too soon can have a potentially damaging effect on young people who may then find it much more difficult to develop all the other aspects of loving relationships, without overt sexuality forming a part of those relationships. In Michael Rutter's words 'pre-marital sex may not be sinful but that does not mean that it is sensible'.

Although we may subscribe to the values behind these arguments, it is clear that social workers often become involved with teenagers who have already had sexual experiences in the past, or who are currently engaged in sexual activity, some of which may have been satisfying, some of which may have been traumatic or frightening. We increase the young person's feelings of guilt and alienation if our attitude is one of disapproval or condemnation. Sadly many residential establishments where teenagers live still adopt this approach where '... a denial of sexuality is still the first refuge, punishment the second...'[6]

Residential workers have a particularly good opportunity to do much in encouraging young people to talk about relationships in ways which enable them to see themselves and others as whole people, and not simply as a sexual person – or any other one-faceted person for that matter. Group discussions – both formal and informal – are a means not only of raising many of the issues surrounding sexuality and relationships, but of helping young people to respond to and support each other in positive, caring ways. This enables them to begin to experience relationships within a group setting where they are accepted, valued and understood, and where they can start to find their own emerging identity.

Margaret Crompton in her book, *Respecting Children*,[7] has written a chapter entitled 'Keep in Touch'. In it she argues that as children grow up in our society, they have less and less physical contact with anyone. As we all have a basic human need for closeness, and this need is increased when people have had a troubled early life, then early sexual exploration and experimentation may appear to be the only available option for troubled teenagers. She says, 'It may be up to the social worker to show that warm places may be found in places and even embraces other than sexual.'

ADOLESCENTS WITH SPECIAL NEEDS

There is a group of adolescents who require special consideration because of their particular difficulties and needs. This is those who have a mental or physical disability which, without sensitive and informed help, may lead to a sexual handicap too. Chiefly this arises because adults who have been caring for them as children experience great difficulty in allowing the child to 'grow up', and find it easier to continue to see them as asexual and dependent.

In many ways this is not surprising. Adolescence, when teenagers are beginning to find their own way in the world and establish their identity as separate from their parents, is a traumatic period for many parents who may suffer feelings of loss and redundancy. When the child is disabled, parents often have to face the fact that their child may never work, may always be dependent, and all their feelings about having given birth to a handicapped child will come to the surface again. To try to avoid the inevitable pain of this, parents and professionals alike will often collude in a denial process.

Wendy Greengross writes, 'Accepting the sexuality of a disabled child is ... difficult and embarrassing, and the common reaction ... is to ignore the subject in the hope that it will go away ... this is part of the Peter Pan syndrome: keep the child child-like and the question of sex will not arise.'[8] There may be a few people who are so severely handicapped that they do not experience sexual urges or arousal, but the majority of disabled people with whom we have contact will experience normal sexual feelings just like anyone else. Helping these people to understand and express their sexuality may at times be our task.

Non-handicapped children find out about sex through play, exploring their own bodies and those of other children – fighting, teasing, touching. Later groups of teenagers share first experiences of disco dances, holding hands, kissing and cuddling. Disabled young people are often denied all these preliminaries, and do not have the same opportunity of testing out one another's responses to early expressions of sexual excitement and awareness. When placed into situations where sexual feelings are 'allowed' this is usually much later in life and the handicapped person may then find himself or herself unprepared for dealing with these feelings.

As social workers we need to recognize first of all the needs of those people – including ourselves – who have the care of handicapped people. We need to create an environment in which carers will be able to talk about their fears and share their pain. Only then will we be able to face the unavoidable pain of those for whom we care in their struggles to achieve satisfying relationships. We cannot protect handicapped people from the ups and downs of relationships without severely restricting their development as human beings. If the feelings which hinder or block our work with handicapped people, or with our son or our daughter, are dealt with, then that opens the way for developing a wide range of creative opportunities for the education, and physical and emotional well-being of those people for whom we seek to care. Exactly how this is to be achieved is beyond the scope of this chapter.

I am convinced that once the need has been identified and accepted with all the emotions it raises, people will be freed to use their own imagination and intimate knowledge of their child, or the group of people for whom they care, to assist them in their search for ways and means of enabling those people to lead happier and more fulfilled lives.

Jean Vanier, founder of L'Arche communities, has spent many years living and working with people who have a mental handicap. His recent book, *Man and Woman He Made Them*[9] will be helpful to all who are engaged in this work.

THE NEEDS OF THE ELDERLY

Something which is often ignored is the subject of the sexual needs and interests of the elderly. It is all too easy for us to assume that all old people accept sexual inactivity in later life. I wonder why we dehumanize people in this way? Admission to hospital or residential accommodation is traumatic enough for someone, without those of us who care for them dictating what we consider to be morally or socially acceptable ways of behaving, saying what can and cannot be allowed, and often this means that most forms of physical contact are not.

We still hear horror stories of husbands and wives not being allowed to even *see* each other, let alone any other relationships being supported. As responsible adults we do have the right to make our views known. We do not have a right to impose our own values onto other people, especially people who have lived a life-time holding different ones. We must respect and accept elderly people as they are and create the opportunities which they need in order to remain in contact with themselves and with others. Inevitably there will be difficulties – especially in residential care where one is working with large numbers of people who may hold conflicting opinions and values. This is where the skills of group living are necessary. Much of our time will be spent in helping people to accept each other, and indeed to respect and value those very differences.

THE RESIDENTIAL WORKER

Residential workers, as I have already suggested, have many opportunities for helping people with their relationships. They are also in particular difficulties because of this. By its very nature residential life is an exposed one where all our actions may be open to interpretation and misinterpretation. We have all seen headlines about workers who have been guilty or accused of sexual misconduct with residents, and some of us know a little of the anguish that can be caused through this.

Peter Righton[10] suggests that residential workers may be so aware of their own vulnerability that this gets passed on to the residents in the form of a 'double deprivation' of first coming into care, and then being deprived of the closeness, tenderness and deep sharing of relationships with their care-givers or with each other. Residential workers and those responsible for them need to give urgent attention to this. Training, staff meetings or discussion groups and supervision are all needed to help individuals work out their own stance, and to provide the support of the team for all its members. In this way positive caring can be achieved.

In a book reflecting many years of residential child care, Pamela Pick asks, '... do not superficial standards get too much attention? There are standards which refer to a much deeper level. When we are assured of our value ... we are no longer like a fortress in a state of siege: we can lower the drawbridge and let in fresh discoveries about ourselves ... Coping with insight is a gradual process, and it is here, at this point of reality, that a child can begin to see aims and set standards.'[11] Perhaps the only standards which are really meaningful for us are those which come from within ourselves.

I am aware that in the main I am merely raising issues here, and not providing any solutions. We do have to find our own way, know ourselves. What is appropriate and right for some individuals and groups may not be acceptable for others. I would suggest that there is nothing wrong with this, provided that those people who are at the centre of our concern, those whom we are endeavouring to help and care for, actually *feel* that this is so. It is much easier to accept someone's limitations and weaknesses if we feel that they genuinely care about us.

Notes

[1]   Michael Rutter, *A Measure of our Values*, Swarthmore Lecture 1983, Quaker Home Service, London.
[2]   Constance Lindemann, 'Sexual Freedom: The Right to Say No,' *Social Casework*, 1983, Family Service Association of America.
[3]   See Note 1.
[4]   Michael Rutter, *op. cit.*
[5]   Jessica Hallam, 'My Heart Belongs to Daddy', *The Listener*, 9 February 1984.
[6]   Leonard Davies, *Sex and the Social Worker*, Heinemann Educational/ *Community Care*, 1983.
[7]   Margaret Crompton, *Respecting Children*, Edward Arnold, 1980.
[8]   Wendy Greengross, *Entitled to Love*, National Marriage Guidance Council, 1976.
[9]   Darton, Longman and Todd, 1985.
[10] Peter Righton, 'Sex and the Residential Social Worker', *Social Work Today*, 15 February 1977.
[11] Pamela Pick, *Children at Treetops*, Residential Care Association, 1981.

CHAPTER 11

Taking Children into Care

Peter Gilbert

'Oh for a good spirit who would take the house-tops off … and show a Christian people what dark shapes issue from amidst their homes to swell the retinue of the Destroying Angel. For only one night's view of the pale phantoms rising from the scenes of our…neglect; and from the thick and sullen air where Vice and Fever propagate together, raining the tremendous social retributions…men, delayed no more… would then apply themselves, like creatures of one common origin, owing one duty to the Father of one family, and tending to one common end, to make the world a better place.'[1]

Social policy and legislation in Britain has, from as far back as the Anglo-Saxon kingdoms, been a seesaw struggle between intervention and *laissez-faire*, care and control. Legislation, because it is an imperfect and imprecise human instrument, has to steer a delicate route between the Scylla of individual liberty and the Charybdis of society's wellbeing.

The quotation at the start of this chapter from Charles Dickens' *Dombey and Son* reflects a growing awareness in his time of the consequences of neglect: that to 'comfort the widow and orphan' and 'succour the fatherless child' were not simply nice biblical aphorisms, but necessary measures to build up a Christian society and to ward off the evils of crime and pestilence, which emanated from the slums built on man's greed.

A CHANGE OF HEART

Children in Dickens' time were considered, in the words of Pip's egregious relatives in *Great Expectations*, to be 'a world of trouble', 'ungrateful' and 'naturally vicious', but gradually a change of heart occurred, through perception and national need, which began to see children as part of the nation's posterity. During the first half of this century, legislation such as the 1933 Children and Young Person's Act started to afford children protection and they began to be seen as individuals in their own right, no longer the property or insurance policy of parents or state. The 1948 Children Act, stemming partly from the sense of one nation created by the second world war, attempted to move away from a model of care based on the Poor Law to one where the state compensated for the loss of opportunity caused by deprivation. The Act was part of a legislative programme designed to create a welfare state, a new Jerusalem out of that 'green and pleasant land', Isaiah's 'fertile hill-side'. Now some commentators see the rise in juvenile crime and drug abuse, and the breakdown of many moral codes and question whether the vinepress has brought forth 'wild grapes' (to use the imagery of Isaiah 5:1-7) and whether the walls of the vineyard should be broken down.

MODERN LEGISLATIVE CHANGES

The 1930 Poor Law Act laid a duty on local authorities to set to work as apprentices those children whose parents could not keep and maintain them. Thus the early part of that decade looked back clearly to the concepts of less eligibility and procreation for national production. As Dickens' character, the beadle, Sownds, pronounces:

> 'We must marry 'em. We must have our national schools to walk at the head of, and we must have our standing armies. We must marry 'em ma'am...and keep the country going.'[2]

The second world war in which a whole people bore the risks and experience of war; the chaos and consequences of evacuation; the division of responsibilities exposed by the tragic death in 1945 of Dennis O'Neill in his foster home; and the Curtis Report's exposition of the effects of institutional care, created the climate of opinion in which the Children Act of 1948 was passed through Parliament. This seminal act with its obligation on local authorities '...to exercise their powers with respect to him (i.e. the child in care) so as to further his best interests, and to afford him the opportunity for the proper development of his character and abilities', meant that a child could be received into care, should he be abandoned or lost, or if his parent or guardian were temporarily or permanently prevented from caring for him at home. The 1933 Children and Young Persons Act had provided for the taking of children into care under a Fit Person Order.

Despite the creation of children's departments in local authorities under the auspices of the Home Office in 1948, there were no powers for the authorities to undertake preventive work with children and their families until the passing of the Children and Young Persons Act 1963. Although this should have produced a diminution of the numbers of children coming into care, such is the ambiguous nature of legislative change, that the numbers increased in the following three years – perhaps due to the increasing numbers being referred to the children's departments[3]. The preventive duties imposed by this Act have caused continuing dilemmas for social workers as these have both moved them into a political arena and made them gatekeepers of scarce resources.

While the 1948 Act had dealt only with deprived children, the prevailing philosophy of the 1960s was that the roots of deprivation and delinquency were the same and this led to the 1969 Children and Young Persons Act, with care proceedings through the juvenile court being used to remove both the 'deprived' and the 'depraved' from the sources of infection. The ethical questions as to whether children benefit more in the end from a 'welfare' or 'justice' approach are alive today, but the move away from a children's service to one serving the family as a whole brought the children's departments to an end, and they were absorbed into the new generic Social Services departments in 1971.[4]

The death of Maria Colwell in 1973 was the *cause célèbre* for the move back towards legislation and service orientation which placed the best interests of the child in the paramount position. Ten years on from the 1975 Children Act, important legislation is still split between several acts of Parliament, despite a consolidating Act in 1980; new legislation stresses the rights of natural parents to have access to the child (under the 1983 Health and Social Services and Social Security Adjudications Act), while a number of the provisions in the 1975 Act have still not been implemented; and there is still a lack of consensus as to what constitutes the best interests of the child.

ROUTES INTO CARE[5]

Child Care Act 1980
Section 2 Voluntary reception into care.
Section 57(b) Closure of a voluntary home - only applies if child appears to be over 17 years.

Children and Young Persons Act 1969
Section 28(1) Place of safety order.
Section 20(1) Interim order.
Section 1(3) Care order following proceedings in which Section 1(2) (a)–(f) have been proved, and the need for an order also shown.

Section 7(7) Care order following proceedings where the child has been found guilty of an offence punishable by imprisonment if committed by an adult.

Section 29(3) Detention in care at the request of the police, pending a court appearance within 72 hours.

Section 23(1) Remand.

Family Law Reform Act 1969

Section 7(2) & (3) Wardship proceedings in the High Court. Care order but the court continues to exercise jurisdiction.

Matrimonial Causes Act 1973

Section 43(1) Divorce proceedings in a county or High Court – care order.

Domestic Proceedings and Magistrates Courts Act 1978

Section 89 Divorce proceedings in a magistrates court – care order.

Foster Children Act 1980

Section 12 Removal from a private foster home on a place of safety order, Section 12(5) applies if child appears to be over 17 years.

Adoption Act 1958

Section 43(3) Removal from an adoptive home (to be Section 34 of the Adoption Act 1976 when implemented) – care order.

Children Act 1975

Section 17(1) (b) Refusal of an adoption order – care order.

Section 36(3) (when implemented). Revocation of a custody order – care order.

Guardianship Act 1973

Section 2(2) (b) Refusal of a guardianship order – care order.

The Ethics of Intervention

Intervening in a family raises many ethical problems. Although the social worker may not always 'take' a child 'into care' through the use of a place of safety order and/or care proceedings in the juvenile court, but rather 'receive' the child under Section 2 of the Child Care Act 1980, through a parent's request, the effect may be just as traumatic for all concerned, and the parent's rights may subsequently be assumed by the local authority even though the original route into care was a voluntary one.

Take the case of Dave (all names are assumed). He became clinically depressed following the death of his wife and found it increasingly difficult to care for his daughter Amy. Dave's anger at his loss was projected onto Amy, and though his local church community were very supportive, their goodwill came under increasing pressure. Eventually Dave was persuaded to accept an informal admission to a psychiatric hospital and Amy was received into care. Counselling with both father and daughter during the separation, a gradual reintroduction and intensive domiciliary support, cemented the relationship while preserving the goodwill of the community's support.

Reception into care can be seen by families in a much less positive light. Dawn was a single mother with an eight-year old son, Christopher. At times of stress and psychiatric breakdown she asked that he should be received into care. She presented these separations as the social services' decision to Christopher, however, so as to shed the blame from herself. In this situation battles took place as a demonstration of Dawn's resistance to parting with her son. In the end these battles acted as a self-fulfilling prophecy when the local authority was forced to assume parental rights to protect Christopher. Through the local authority clarifying its position, this decision helped both mother and son and eventually led to a successful reunion.

The morality of intervening in family situations is never simple and raises many personal feelings in the worker himself. The balance of the child's, parent's and society's rights is delicately poised and much depends on the confluence between society's attitude as expressed through legislation, the culture in which the family is placed, and the worker's personal beliefs. One writer has expressed it in this way: 'Social work operates on the boundaries between public and private life, depending on the resources of informal as well as formal care.'[6]

THE CHURCH AND THE FAMILY

Christians of all traditions would agree that the family is the foundation of society:

'a family ideally is a society in which all bear common pain and share common grief and all give and receive equally of love.'[7]

'The family has received from God its mission to be the first and vital cell of society.'[8]

'...not only a school for heaven; in a certain sense it is the anticipated Kingdom of God itself.'[9]

...ily is not something separate from society but
... within it, the family unit having bonds with others
...immediate family and kin as part of a new community
...ed heart and soul.'

In New Testament terms, Paul made an analogy between the relationship of man and wife and Christ's union with his Church. Each Christian is united to Christ, the central vine (in the picture language of John's Gospel), and is bound through him to all his fellows so that in union with Christ we 'form one body, and as parts of it we belong to each other', in the words of Romans 12.

In that they look outward towards the creation of a brotherhood the Christian and sociological approaches have much in common. The Anglican theologian and moral philosopher G. R. Dunstan [10] defines the functions of the family as

1. *Biological* to perpetuate the human race within a stable framework.
2. *Emotional* meeting emotional needs of family members of different ages.
3. *Economic* to meet the basic needs of life.
4. *Social* to prepare us for citizenship.
5. *Cultural* imparting fundamental beliefs and values.

Clare Winnicott, one of the most influential of a generation of child care workers, says much the same when she speaks of preserving the natural family whenever possible and finding alternative families if this is not possible. For Winnicott, the basic principles underlying this approach are that 'the basic social unit on which the stability of the individual rests is the family' and 'family life constitutes the natural link between the individual and society'. [11]

Where Christians might diverge from the sociological approach is in regarding the changes which education and industrialization have brought to bear on family responsibilities. Ronald Fletcher, [12] in his standard textbook *The Family and Marriage in Britain*, shows how functions such as health care, recreation, education and even religion – have been appropriated by various 'professional' agencies, thus transferring the traditional family functions.

Many Christians feel uneasy about this trend and wonder whether welfare principles do not in the end both weaken the position of the family and become the wedge for increasing state regulation and control. [13] Karl Rahner sums it up like this:

'The principle is that the state as such, without actually becoming a "night watchman" of mere legality, must, precisely in the area of social institutions, set in motion on its own initiative only that which the free individual groups within that society cannot perform themselves.'[14]

Another source of contention is that of the concept of 'love'. John Bowlby's seminal work *Child Care and the Growth of Love*[15], gives overwhelming predominance to the mother-child relationship, but recent critics, such as Patricia Morgan in her book *Delinquent Fantasies*[16], have suggested that it is the retreat of adults from the world of children, from their responsibility to be adult, and the emasculation of the father, that is the prime source of the juvenile delinquency which is so prevalent. As social worker and author, John Stroud, put it: 'This is the age of the weak dad.' God, both through his prophets and his Son, has made clear that both conditional and unconditional love[17] are vital to our human development. The Mother-God who would have even more compassion on us than the woman with her 'sucking child' (Isaiah 49:15), is also the Father-God who shows just anger if our deeds are evil (Micah 3 : 4).

THE FAMILY IN CRISIS

Although pessimistic commentators have written obituaries on the family for many years, there is no doubt that events over the past fifty years have placed increasing strain on family cohesion. The dislocation of a nation at war, of industrialization and decline, of rehousing, of divorce, have all played a part in disrupting family life, while government policy has given the impression of lending support while often undermining it. Recent legislation on maintenance has placed women in the double-bind of being advised to retain a family-orientated role while needing to work to provide for themselves should the family disintegrate.

In the industrial field there is a dichotomy in the political thinking of the 'new right' which advocates a high degree of labour mobility and yet deplores the decline of the extended family. This contradiction exists in Marxist thinking also, as Marx and Engels urged the working classes to become more mobile, sell their labour at the highest price and escape from 'rural idiocy'.

Housing policies under both Labour and Conservative administrations have conspired to imprison, not free, those they were meant to serve. The tower blocks are monuments to human folly. The rehousing described by Wilmott and Young in *Family and Kinship in East London*[18] in London in the 1950s broke up supportive families ('if you're with your family you've always got someone to help you'). The slum clearance in towns like Brighton in the 1930s merely shifted the slums to less accessible and more stigmatized suburban estates, leaving valuable central town sites to be occupied by the symbols of the state – police station and law courts; and of commercial capitalism – the credit card emporium of American Express.[19]

Although marriage is still popular, a quarter of marr[...]nd in divorce[20] and one in five children born today will w[...]eir parents' divorce before they reach the age of sixteen. [...]er of one-parent families has increased from 8.3% in the 1970[...] 12%, with the biggest group of single mothers in the 16-24 age-range[21]. In 1971 there were 515,000 single-parent families; by 1981 there were 916,000. Single parents are more at risk of losing their children to the state, and Gingerbread – an organization existing for single parents – told the Barclay Report that it advised its members to have no dealings with social workers.[22] But for the social work profession the burden of supervising children of broken marriages, imposed by orders through the matrimonial courts, is increasing all the time.

The latest NSPCC survey[23] quotes marital discord and unemployment as two prime factors in abusing families. Babies born to working-class families are more vulnerable than those in higher socio-economic groups; but state income maintenance, the National Health Service and education facilities are all slanted towards or more accessible to the rich. As LeGrand has stated: 'Almost all public expenditure in the Social Services in Britain benefits the better off to a greater extent than the poor.'[24]

These factors should give social workers pause for thought in their attitude to poor families if Seebohm's concept of 'a community-based and family-orientated service...available to all' is not to become the social policing of the disadvantaged.

BREAKING THE BONDS THAT TIE

The blood tie is one of the most ancient of human concepts. Although Sophocles' *Oedipus Rex* is best known in connection with Freud's exposition of latent sexuality, the essential story, however, is about adoption and, in Oedipus' words, 'to unravel the mystery of my birth' and to 'know who I am'.

Most children at some stage wonder about their genealogical identity and measure up their looks, mannerisms and personality with those of their parents to seek reassurance about their right to belong. Adopted children who have no knowledge or uncertain knowledge about their natural parents can suffer from what is called 'genealogical bewilderment'.[25]

At the time of the Maria Colwell inquiry in 1974, social workers were accused of putting too high a value on the 'blood tie', and the publication of books such as Goldstein, Freud and Solnit's *Beyond the Best Interests of the Child* [26] supported this claim. Research into the views of children in care showed that many were impatient for a definite plan of action, for placement with a substitute family if they couldn't return home, and protection of that placement. As one child said, 'It's not who borned you that matters but who loves you'[27].

In the decade following the 1975 Children Act, designed to secure a better future for children's interests, the tide has turned towards parental rights and there is now a danger that social workers will prevaricate over long-term planning for children, despite the evidence that children who are in care for longer than six months have only a one-in-four chance of leaving care before the age of sixteen,[28] and the complementary evidence that when natural ties have been broken, even in the case of older children, adoption can still provide the security that the child craves.[29]

CHILDREN IN CARE

Year	1961	1974	1977	1981	1982
Total	62,200	91,300	100,000	96,900	93,200

While a 'tug of love' between natural and substitute parents persists in social policy and law, section 26 of the Children Act 1975 permits adopted children over the age of eighteen years to have access to their birth records. Few attempt to trace their natural parents, but many find a need, as a modern author puts it 'to travel the bureaucratic road to identity', '...these displaced persons whose umbilical cord' is 'a court order'[30].

For the Christian the cosmic identity of individuals is of supreme importance. We cannot say like Sophocles that 'the generations of mortal man adds up to nothing', for we know that: 'When the fullness of time was come, God sent forth His Son, made of a woman...that we might receive adoption as sons...and as a son, then an heir of God through Christ.'[31]

SUFFER THE CHILDREN

> 'Ha!' said Dr Blimber, 'shall we make a man of him?' 'I had rather be a child,' replied Paul.[32]

Although there are more vivid descriptions of children in Dickens, none of his novels describes better than *Dombey and Son* the way that adults can treat children as their property. Until the last few decades children were the goods and chattels of their parents and it has only slowly emerged as a legal principle that the child's interests should be considered in their own right and that children should be given separate legal representation in court proceedings.

Many children in care now feel, however, that they are the chattels of social workers. The *cause célèbre* of Graham Gaskin, in care to Liverpool Council for many years, shows the pent-up anger of people who feel that the local authority took over the rights and duties of parents only to come up with no long-term parental aim. As one young adult leaving care put it: 'I thought they had all sorts of rotten plans about what should happen to me and I was bloody angry because they wouldn't tell me. When I got older I realised that nobody actually had any plans at all. That hurt and made me even more angry.'[33]

Good practice is not ended at the time of the *decision* whether to receive a child into care, remove him from danger, or take proceedings in court. It extends to local authorities resisting the temptation to close long-established children's homes for financial reasons; social service departments ending degrading practices such as use of the clothing order book; and above all to the need to listen to the individual child: 'To ascertain as far as practicable the wishes and feelings of the child and give due consideration to them, having regard to his age and understanding,' as Section 18 of the 1980 Child Care Act puts it.

Perhaps it is also important for parents and social workers to seek forgiveness from children, and for children, at whatever stage, to forgive for 'the sanctification of the parents.'[34]

THE HEALING OF HARMS

Christian thinking has changed with that of society's in general in regard to the balance between parents' and children's rights. Although a document such as the Catholic Church's *Charter of the Rights of the Family* lays stress on the state's need to respect parental choice in education,[35] it also seeks an equilibrium between the state's duty to safeguard children and respect for the natural rights of parents[36]. In like manner the charter of the British Association of Social Workers asserts:

'Children's rights and needs do not exist in a vacuum. They are bound up with those of their parents ... While children's rights and parent's rights are intirely complementary and to a large extent indivisible, parental rights are *not* rights of possession and they do not take precedence over a child's right to an upbringing which will promote his emotional, physical, social and intellectual well-being.'[37]

The Christian perspective is that legislation and social policy should reflect support for families fulfilling their natural responsibilities. Should the state be required to step in in order to protect children it must ensure that it can provide better for the child's needs than the parent could[38].

The *Report on the Death of Shirley Woodcock* (1984) makes the point that cuts in services can mean that children in society's care, placed with substitute parents, can suffer injury and even death. It is not encouraging that a foster child can die so many years after Dennis O'Neill, the *cause célèbre* which gave impetus to the founding of the child care service.

The Christian approach has much in common with that outlined by Margaret Adcock, in *Rights of Children*[39]. The Christian social worker should attempt to preserve the natural family and the kinship network wherever possible, but if separation is unavoidable, then decisions about a permanent placement should be made within a defined space of time. Children should not be displaced or allowed to drift in care, as they cannot invest in transient relationships, and 'bureaucratic love' is not enough. In his second letter to the Thessalonians, Paul warns us not just to be people 'who do nothing but meddle in other people's business'. As Augustine advises, the worker should see 'Right Order' as 'first, that he harm no one, and, second that he help whomever he can.'[40]

It is to be hoped that the Swedish model of massive State intervention[41] will never be the model in Britain, and that the integration of child care law and practice advocated by the 1984 Short Report will produce an equipoise of welfare and justice that will see law enlightened by love for: 'love does no harm to his neighbour: therefore love is the fulfilling of the Law.'[42]

Notes

[1] Charles Dickens, *Dombey and Son*.
[2] *Dombey and Son*.
[3] See C. Wendelken, *Children In and Out of Care*, Heinemann Educational/*Community Care*, 1983.
[4] See J. Packman, *The Child's Generation*, Blackwell and Robertson, 1975.
[5] Taken with permission from *Children In and Out of Care*, see Note 3 above.
[6] R. Pinker, 'How it seems to me', *Community Care*, 5 April 1984.
[7] 1958 Lambeth Conference.
[8] *Decree on the Apostolate of the Laity*, Second Vatican Council, 1966.
[9] Larry Christensen, *The Christian Family*, Kingsway 1970.
[10] G.R. Dunstan, *The Family is not Broken*, SCM, 1962.
[11] Clare Winnicott, *Child Care and Social Work*, Bookstall Publication, 1964.
[12] R. Fletcher, *The Family and Marriage in Britain*, Penguin 1973.
[13] See P. Coman, *Catholics and the Welfare State*, Longman, 1972.
[14] Karl Rahner, 'Practical Theology and Social Work in the Church', *Theological Investigations*, Vol. 10, Darton, Longman and Todd, 1971.
[15] John Bowlby, *Child Care and the Growth of Love*, Penguin, 1953.
[16] Patricia Morgan, *Delinquent Fantasies*, Temple Smith, 1978.
[17] See Eric Fromm, *The Art of Loving*, Unwin, 1968.
[18] Wilmott and Young, *Family and Kinship in East London*, Routledge and Kegan Paul, 1957.
[19] See P. Dickens and P. Gilbert, *The State and the Housing Question*, University of Sussex monograph, 1979.
[20] See *Families in Focus*, Study Commission on the Family, 1983.
[21] *General Household Survey 1982*, HMSO, 1984.
[22] Barclay Report, *Social Workers: Their Roles and Tasks*, National Institute for Social Work/Bedford Square Press, 1982.
[23] National Society for the Prevention of Cruelty to Children, *Trends in Child Abuse*, 1984.
[24] J. LeGrand, *The Strategy of Equality*, Allen and Unwin, 1982.
[25] See H.J. Sants, 'Genealogical Bewilderment in Children with Substitute Parents', *Child Adoption*, British Agencies for Adoption and Fostering, undated.
[26] Goldstein, Freud and Solnit, *Beyond the Best Interests of the Child*, Free Press, 1973.
[27] Quoted in R. Page and G. Clark, *Who Cares?*, National Children's Bureau, 1977.
[28] J. Rowe and L. Lambert, *Children Who Wait*, Association of British Adoption Agencies, 1973.
[29] See C.R. Smith, *Adoption and Fostering: Why and How*, Macmillan/BASW, 1984.
[30] P. D. James, *Innocent Blood*, Faber 1980.
[31] Galatians 4:3-7

32 Charles Dickens, *Dombey and Son*.
33 Quoted in R. Parker, *Planning for Deprived Children*, National Children's Home, 1971
34 John Paul II, *Familiaris Consortio*, 1981.
35 Catholic Church, *Charter of the Rights of the Family*, October 1983 Article 5.
36 As above, Article 4.
37 Quoted from *Social Work Today*, 29 March 1977.
38 See R. Watson, 'The Best Interests of the Child', *British Journal of Social Work*, Autumn 1976.
39 Margaret Adcock, *Rights of Children*, British Agencies for Adoption and Fostering.
40 Augustine, *City of God*, Book XIX.
41 'Spectre of Children's Gulag Haunts Sweden', *The Observer*, 19 August 1984.
42 Romans 13:10.

CHAPTER 12

The Ethics of Industrial Action

David Lane

To strike or not to strike is a question which thousands of social workers, residential workers, nursery nurses and others in the personal social services have had to face in the last few years. There are no easy solutions to the question, and the answers people have found have caused a lot of agony. While this chapter looks at the issues involved from a Christian perspective, the questions which non-Christians ask of themselves cover the same ground and the wish to find a just way of dealing with industrial relations is in no sense the moral preserve of the Christian.

Withdrawal of labour, or strike action, provides the most clearcut example of conflicts of interest between employers, managers, workers, clients and the public, and is therefore used as the focus for this chapter. In a less dramatic form, though, the same questions underlie many other problems in industrial relations in the personal social services generally, and their impact may be just as serious, resulting for example in loss of morale and commitment on the part of staff and consquently poorer service for clients.

For people wishing to apply Christian thinking in practice, one of the most fundamental problems of religious belief is posed squarely by industrial action. On the one hand, some religious teaching is absolute and demanding and clearcut; on the other, especially when the teaching is applied to everyday life, it is relative and non-directive and unclear. There are plenty of examples of the absolute demands of Jesus' teaching in the New Testament. In the Sermon on the Mount, recorded in Matthew's Gospel, the values of the kingdom Jesus was establishing were laid out. 'Love your enemies... If a man wants to sue you for your coat, let him have it, and your overcoat as well. If anybody forces you to go a mile with him, do more—go two miles with him. Give to the man who asks anything from you, and don't turn away from the man who wants to borrow.'

In Luke's Gospel, Jesus approved as the essential law by which people should live: 'Thou shalt love the Lord thy God with all thy heart and with all thy soul and with all thy strength and with all thy mind – and thy neighbour as thyself.' When questioned about what was meant by 'neighbour', he gave the example of the Good Samaritan who put himself at personal risk and major inconvenience to help a person who had been a traditional enemy, when those who might have been expected to help had failed to do so.

Both the teaching and the parable are clearcut and perhaps somewhat simplified, as one would expect in religious documents intended to make teaching-points clear. The Christian is expected to put the needs of others (including those of adversaries) first, and to put himself at risk if necessary in the process. This demand is unequivocal, and has historically underlain the motivation of monastic orders, missionary societies and the thinking of many professional groups. This approach is clearly at odds with any thought of industrial action to improve the lot of the Christian who is in a serving role.

Jesus himself set an example to his followers by choosing a course of action which led to his own death, a sacrifice to save others. To the Christian, Jesus' death on the cross and his resurrection represent more than an example. It is also a means, indicating that evil and death can be overcome, and that life, as represented by Jesus, triumphs.

This may seem several stages removed from industrial action. The link is that people are motivated to undertake their work for many reasons, but if their motivation is destroyed or damaged, the quality of their work will also be seriously affected. In so far as Christians work under a command to be of service to others, their beliefs are of critical importance to them, and they will not want to compromise their beliefs. The same will be true of any person motivated by strong personal convictions. Even where there is no strong motivation, the need to rationalize hurt done to dependent clients by strike action itself stultifies professional sensitivity.

The problem faced by Christians is that, even if their teaching is clearcut and the parables point to only one way of acting in the situation, it is far from clear how to *apply* the teaching when the problems of daily living have to be tackled. Instead of obvious black and white issues, we tend to find a confusion of shades of grey, with some shapes emerging from the fog to indicate possible ways forward.

THE COMPLEX WEB OF CONSEQUENCES

Much Christian teaching in the New Testament deals with people as individuals and how they relate immediately to other individuals. In everyday life, however, we are members of a complex society both nationally and in our immediate surroundings. We have complicated networks of relationships, and our actions may at times even have consequences for other people we may never meet. As individuals we may be professional social care workers, employees of agencies which make demands upon us, members of trades unions, members of our families, adherents to political parties, holders of religious beliefs, and so on. These allegiances may well at times conflict, and we have to sort out the relative priority of the demands made upon us by the different groups with which we identify.

A parent has duties to his family, for example, and if an employer is exploiting him as a worker, he may feel that he is justified in taking industrial action to obtain a fair wage for the sake of his family, even if he had been prepared to accept poverty in serving others himself. The same question applies less obviously to the time people dedicate to their service of others, and to their involvement of their families in the work. The celibacy of the priesthood simplifies this issue by preventing competing claims of this type from the start, and the demands made upon ministers' wives clearly demonstrate the problem. Less well documented is the impact on social workers' partners when disturbed clients telephone constantly, or the effect on resident staff's children of living with difficult and delinquent children. In short, while the Christian (or non-Christian) worker may be prepared to put clients before his own needs, he may at times have to make comparative judgements about clients' needs and the needs of others he serves, such as his family.

The second problem of relativity is that the commandment instructs people to love their neighbours as themselves, and the clear corollary is that people need to have concern for themselves as well. Despite the overwhelming needs Jesus had to face, he still took time out to be alone and think, and he was criticized for enjoying himself too much at parties. Similarly, people today have their own needs to think of. If their pay and conditions are so abysmal that they suffer, how do the needs of staff stand in relation to clients'? On a relative basis, there may well be justification for taking industrial action to ensure that one is treated as well as one's neighbour, if only so that one may serve him efficiently.

Thirdly, even if the social care worker always places service to the client as the highest priority, there may be some doubt as to how this is best achieved. If budgets or staffing ratios are so appalling that clients suffer, it can be argued that it is in the interests of the clients (or, at least, those that will follow) if they suffer now for the sake of improvements later, and the staff may feel that industrial action will draw their clients' plight to the attention of employers and managers. Furthermore, any crisis which has reached the point of strike action is likely to have been preceded by a history of breakdown in communication, mismanagement, failure and grounds for recrimination and self-justification.

In issues of this type, the absolute moral instructions are buried under a welter of relativities. It may be argued that whatever is most effective in achieving the goal becomes the most moral line of action; pragmatism becomes the good and right. The danger then is that any means becomes acceptable to achieve the desired end.

It is possible to obtain certain goals through exerting emotional pressures, through violence, or through manipulating procedures. Pragmatically judged, these measures may succeed but can also backfire. Ethically evaluated, some of the lines of action may be as unloving to other 'neighbours' as the failure to achieve improvements to clients may be to them. Industrial action, for example, to keep a unit open may help the clients it serves at the expense of others who lose the benefit of reallocated resources. In these complexities there is no clear guideline or rule of thumb.

THE INDIVIDUAL AND THE GROUP

Faced with these circumstances, each person clearly carries the responsibility to make up their own mind and to act as an independent individual. As stated earlier, most Christian teaching is aimed at people as individuals, seeking their own salvation and atonement, their own personal understanding of life and relationship with God.

We are all members of other groups, however, and we behave not just as individuals in those groups but as group members, displaying characteristics of the group and identifying with its views. People in football crowds commit acts of violence quite out of character with their normal behaviour as individuals; Christians repeat creeds to indicate their solidarity with others even though not everyone may personally identify with every recited belief; social care workers take industrial action at times as part of a movement larger than themselves when they would not have done so as individuals. Such behaviour is normal social conduct, and not simply lapses on the part of the individual.

Action of this type is of course only taken as a result of individuals identifying with it. At times it is hard to resist group pressures, and the peer group pressure of collective solidarity is so powerful and overriding that it has led, for example, to demands for closed shops in many industries. A Christian is expected to be answerable to his conscience; a professional person is expected to hold autonomous standards of conduct and carry individual responsibility. However, if these expectations require the individual to stand out against the group, for example in declining to take industrial action, the possible consequences for relationships between colleagues and rifts in staff teams have also to be considered. There are points at which people have to take stands, but everyone, including their families and clients, may suffer for it long after the industrial action is over.

Individuals may therefore find themselves trapped into situations in which there appears to be no right answer, even with careful thinking and negotiation with the parties involved. During the residential workers' industrial action in 1983, a deputy officer in charge felt that she should not participate in her colleagues' strike action and leave the children unattended. She was aware, however, that any attempt on her part to maintain consistency of care for the children by working with the agency staff who were being taken on in place of the strikers would only lead to escalated industrial action by her colleagues, subsequent ostracism for herself, a rift in the staff team and a model of split parenting to reinforce any similar unhappy relationships experienced by the children before coming into care. There appeared to be no right answer.

The dilemma facing staff in this type of situation is comparable to that of Christians who do not wish to make war and kill but find themselves citizens in countries where it is expected of them. They may feel equal unease as to whether the war can be justified, and there may be no right answer which enables them to satisfy their principles and the expectations laid upon them. Any answer has to be an unhappy compromise which in ethical terms is only partly justifiable. Acceptance of this situation may itself make the resulting decision more tolerable.

POLARIZATION AND NEGOTIATION

Indeed, one of the fundamental problems faced in industrial relations is its polarizing and adversarial nature. It tends to split people into opposing camps when previously they worked as a team, and when subsequently they will need to become a team once more.

The current pattern may well have developed from a genuinely adversarial system of bargaining. In the days when mill owners wrangled with mill workers, each party knew that they were ultimately inter-dependent for success and therefore could not push things too far without damaging themselves, so that compromise resulted. The adversarial model may have been too simple even then, with the consumers of the mills' outputs and the impact of the dispute on local communities to consider.

Certainly the model is inappropriate to social care services now. Negotiations concerning pay and conditions in the statutory sector take place at national level between professional union negotiators and representatives of employing bodies. If industrial action is taken by staff in the form of strike action, the brunt is borne by their clients whom they are paid and motivated to help, not hurt, and by their immediate colleagues, including line managers, who have to stand in for them and who may well be members of the same union. The employers, as distinct from the managers, remain untouched by such action.

Tom O'Brien MP drew up criteria for a just strike. Of these the fifth was that 'consideration must be given to the harm done to innocent parties and essential services'. In the personal social services, withdrawal of essential services to innocent and vulnerable parties is the only real weapon.

In short, the negotiating system is remote from the work, and industrial action is inevitably misdirected. Furthermore, since the clients of social care workers are themselves weak and incapable of making their voices heard effectively, industrial action in the personal social services has little bite. In short, looking back over the bitter wrangles of the miners' strike in Britain in 1984, if that strike and all its consequences could be survived for a year, then social care workers have little chance of making any impact.

A NEW MODEL?

It might, therefore, be argued that both social care staff and their clients are in weak positions, reliant upon the willingness of employers to accept their moral right to reasonable levels of pay, and unfortunately this has at times led to feelings of exploitation.

Perhaps the root of the problem is that the adversarial system of negotiation is now out of date. It seems that other parties need to be involved to reflect the reality of the situation. Indeed, the people most affected are clients. If they, or their spokesmen, were given a real voice in negotiations, they themselves could indicate the value they feel should be placed upon the staff who serve them. Equally, if representatives of other earning groups were involved in negotiations they could indicate what comparative value should be placed upon social care in relation to other types of work.

Applied widely, such an approach would offer a safety valve where working groups and consumers had to make clear to each other their competing claims for rewards. Any group wishing to gain benefits would learn if it was obtaining wider support in the community or whether it was standing alone.

How does this proposal relate to ethical considerations of industrial action from a Christian viewpoint? For a start, it indicates the need to question accepted practice. The conflict facing social care workers challenged to take industrial action and harm their clients is one that should not need to be put to them, and society should be able to find a way of resolving such impasses without clients or staff suffering. By centring their thinking on the fundamental commandments and beliefs which they should be working out in their social care practice, Christians should be able to free themselves from the blinkers of the *status quo*, the current bureaucratic systems and the accepted political philosophies. 'Liberation theology' is being applied to the political scene in many countries where people feel oppressed; it can also be applied to the more mundane and less dramatic scene of industrial relations in social care. If workers' thinking is rooted in more fundamental beliefs and aims, they will not be enslaved to more superficial considerations, and they will feel free to contemplate fundamental changes, as long as they serve their ultimate goals. It is necessary to interrelate personal beliefs, attitudes, professional thinking and practice. Although the examples used in this chapter are Christian beliefs and industrial action, the need to think through issues and search for consistency between all these aspects of one's functioning applies just as much to non-Christians, and also to other types of action.

A return to fundamental values, analyzing and testing them and then reapplying them to our current situation, can produce new ways of looking at situations. We can be freed of assumptions that accepted methods are the only ones. There is a real opportunity and responsibility to find new answers, and overcome difficulties, consistent with Christian thinking on renewal and liberation.

In the meantime, Christians will continue to find themselves in situations where they refuse to take industrial action on the grounds of their beliefs, and create unhappy tensions in consequence, in situations where they take action and feel they have compromised their beliefs.

Indeed, even if the system changes, social care will continue to present conflicting demands, and the resulting tensions ought perhaps to be seen as challenging opportunities for creative thinking and action. Certainly, no belief system will ever give answers to all problems, and life would be boring if it did.

Industrial action in social care may seem a minor issue on the national scene, but in it can be seen a microcosm of the way we see ourselves, our dependent fellow men and our society. Ultimately, people seek justice in industrial relations, and in society as a whole, so 'that each may care for all, and all may care for each,' as Archbishop William Temple put it. The search for justice is a dynamic process in which it is the seeking that is important rather than the arriving, and the goal is a beacon to give us direction.

CHAPTER 13

Values

Terry Philpot

It is a recorded historical fact that the origin of much social work lies in the work of the church or the inspiration of individual Christians. Furthermore, the religious impulses that have led many social workers to enter their profession are a commonplace. Ordained clergy of different denominations, or those who began ordination studies before switching to social work as a full-time calling, are by no means rare. This is as true of local authority social services as of the voluntary sector.

There is even a suggestion that, at times, social work has been seen as a kind of secular substitute for Christianity. L.E. Elliott Binns refers to this when writing of nineteenth-century thought: 'Some of those who gave themselves up to social work did so in a way of escape from the difficulties which they felt in regard to Christianity as a doctrinal system'.[1] C.S. Loch, active in the Charity Organisation Society at the end of the nineteenth century, and reflecting perhaps the spirit of others in society who formed the Secular Sunday Schools Movement and the Ethical Churches, went so far as to speak of 'a church of charity' when referring to organized forms of caring. Something of this is reflected in Kay McDougall's statement in 1970 which said that to be a professional is to choose not just an occupation but a distinctive way of life that will be judged 'by how we are seen to behave towards clients and towards each other'.[2]

The affinity, then, between Christianity and social work makes it useful to consider those points of departure and confluence between their respective world-views and consequent expectations; for there will be times when a Christian social worker may experience a tension between the world as experienced in his professional life and his own professional insights and those understandings which derive from his faith. What follows cannot claim to be an exhaustive list of all the issues, nor even an exhaustive treatment of those considered. This chapter is best seen as a reflection and a prompt to further thought, study and investigation.

SOCIAL WORK VALUES

Before looking at the values which social work claims to hold, it is necessary to consider what social work is, and not least the difficulty in defining it which continues to bedevil any discussion.

Martin Davies defines social work by stating what it does and by drawing attention to the particular elements which characterize it.[3] These are gatekeeping and resource allocation; supervising, 'often in a rather nominal fashion', specified persons on behalf of the community; providing compensatory care facilities; attempting to change people's attitudes and social circumstances; and, 'above all', contributing to the maintenance and growth of those citizens seen to be deprived and underprivileged, and trying to enrich the lives of those on the margins of society. This list is neither exhaustive nor uncontroversial. Davies underpins these points by writing that 'a *fundamental* belief in the capacity of Man to improve his own circumstances without necessarily doing so at the expense of others is *central* to the social worker's philosophy of practice' (my italics).[4]

Another attempt at definition was given in the Barclay Report, *Social Workers: Their Role and Tasks*.[5] The committee did much the same as Davies by looking to a descriptive definition of social work, while using the words 'formal' and 'informal' as distinguishing prefixes according to where and by whom what it called social work was practised. Formal referred to the paid, professional sector, informal to the work carried out by neighbours and friends.

The most radical dissenting view from the Barclay's 'community social work' was stated by Professor Robert Pinker of the London School of Economics in his note of dissent to the report when he equated social work with casework. This is a much narrower view of what social work is, but one which has long held sway in professional thinking. One reaction to Pinker is to ask how we define all the many other things which social workers do, if his narrow definition is to be accepted.

Statements of definition have traditionally varied from the modest to the grandiose, so that, for example, the *Notes on the Ethics of Social Work*, published by the Association of Social Workers in 1953, stated: 'A social worker is one who, by education, vocation and training, has fitted himself for professional employment in agencies working for the happiness and stability of the individual in the community.' The chairman, Principal Nicholson, stated that 'the social worker's claim to professional status centres upon being a specialist in human relationships, an individual trained and disciplined in human adjustments.'[6]

Barbara Wootton, in her seminal work *Social Science and Social Pathology* offers a view from the other end of the spectrum when she says that the requirements of the social worker are 'good manners, ability and willingness to listen, and efficient methods of record keeping', along with an accurate knowledge of the workings of the services in carrying out what Barbara Wootton seems to define almost as a technical task.[7]

There are others who have suggested that social work is defined by what a social worker does, or (negatively) that it is those things which other professions – the police, medicine, the law – do not do. Or, again, social work has been defined by the statutory work laid upon practitioners. More recently Smith and van Krieken concluded: 'Various social work theorists keep trying to construct a generalised model of social work practice, despite the diversity of social work practices, the main result being that practising social workers are thrown onto their own "intuition", "practice" wisdom or the theory "built into" their workplace.'[8]

It is this lack of an agreed definition about social work which has frustrated attempts to construct a generally agreed theory of social work, resulting in the commonly acknowledged fact that social work as no *unique* set of values. This is not to say, of course, that it lacks values; only that what it has have been borrowed from others, or are shared with others. Noel Timms, in his *Social Work Values: An Enquiry* found this to be the case.[9] The 1976 enquiry by the Central Council for Education and Training in Social Work, *Values in Social Work*, said that it could not define 'value' because of the difficulties which included the effect of being trained in different disciplines, the different views of the nature of social work, and the different personal, moral and political views held by practitioners.

Many would agree that the most generally accepted and usable list of values underlying social work are those stated by Felix Biestek in his *The Casework Relationship*.[10] These have proved durable because they have, for the most part, outlasted the decline in casework. However, they are not beyond question. For example, self-determination for some clients would be regarded as questionable on occasions; confidentiality may be open to interpretation; acceptance may not be possible in group situations; and individualization cannot be seen in total isolation from the rest of the community. (Biestek's other principles are purposeful expression of feelings; a controlled emotional involvement; and a non-judgemental attitude.)

Zofia Butrym, who is both a Christian and a social work teacher, has suggested that whatever the particular model of social work practised, the key social work values would be respect for others, a recognition of 'man's uniqueness', and a belief in the human capacity for change, growth and betterment.[11]   ① RESPECT

SOCIAL WORK VALUES AND CHRISTIAN VALUES

While social work enshrines certain values, one of its most central values – sometimes called respect for persons – is not derived from the social sciences at all, but is, in essence, a religious value, having its justification in a transcendental view of life. Bertrand Russell himself stated: 'If we seek justification for believing in the sacred rights of human beings to be respected as persons having intrinsic value, we must seek it in the higher religions, for we cannot find it in science.'[12] Raymond Plant, summarizing Kant's philosophy in his book, *Social and Moral Theory in Casework*, says: 'A man deserves respect as a potential moral agent in terms of his transcendal characteristic, not because of a particular conjunction of empirical qualities which he might possess. Traits of character might command admiration and other such responses, but respect is owed to a man, irrespective of what he does, because he is a man.'[13]

Thus, the indispensible element in the relationship between social worker and client – respect for the person – comes from a transcendental or supranatural view of humankind. In some ways, respect for the person, arising from the 'uniqueness of man', to take Butrym's phrase, may be said to underlie all other values. It is quite possible to believe in a non-judgemental attitude toward clients, or in the worth and uniqueness of the person without being a Christian or having any religious belief, but the story of the fall and the redemption offers the strongest possible basis for their acceptance. For the fall tells us of our own failings as well as those of others and the redemption speaks of the value God places on us and the possibility of change and renewal.

But whereas social work may be regarded as organized caring or a practical application of ethics, Christianity is not an ethical system, nor can its founder be seen simply as 'a great teacher', 'the ideal man'. This is where ethical humanism and Christian humanism part company. One of the reasons why Christianity has been seen simply as an ethical system is because the word 'Christian' has been used commonly as a synonym for 'good'. To say that someone 'leads a Christian life' if they do not regard themselves as Christians is both insulting to them and shows a curious blindness to the fact that people lead good and exemplary lives with no reference to

Christianity or any religion for that matter.

Christianity is about the restored relationship of humankind with God through the life, death and resurrection of Christ. It is about the call to each man and woman as an individual and in community with others. The kingdom is much more than the sum of its parts, but is a whole community.

However, as J. B. Phillips says in *Making Men Whole*[14], the writers of the New Testament epistles never regarded Christianity as an ethic. For them it was the invasion of the Holy Spirit into their lives so that they might become something else; they were, indeed, transfigured. What was exhibited in their lives was not a performance to please an external God but the manifestation of something new in them and the world. Oscar Wilde in *De Profundis* says: 'Christ does not really teach one anything, but being brought into his presence one becomes something. And everybody is predestined to his presence. Once at least in his life every man walks with Christ to Emmaus.' John says in his first letter: 'Love will come to its perfection in us when we can face the day of judgement without fear; because even in this world we have become as he is,'[15] while Phillips' own translation says that this assurance comes from our knowing 'that our own life in this world is actually his lived in us'.

And so the Samaritan's good works described by Jesus in the well-known parable are not the same as Christian love, as described in the New Testament by Paul. The Samaritan 'had pity' upon the man at the roadside. He cared for him when others went by; he paid the innkeeper to look after the man when he himself had to go. There is little enough of the Samaritan's actions in this world but it is a parable not of how we should act or of acceptance – for it was the Samaritan who was the social pariah, not the victim – but an instructive lesson about whom we may find to be our brother at times of difficulty, of unexpected places where we may find good.

The love which Paul refers to is not pity or good works (though indeed he commends both), but self-giving, loving until it hurts. This is the emotion of which Shakespeare writes when he says that 'love is not love which alters when it alteration finds.' This is the virtue required of the social worker with some of the most unhappy, disturbed and distressed of clients, which allows him to stay with them. Feelings of pity in such circumstances are transformed, so that a new level of understanding, of vulnerability on the part of the helper is reached. Coventry Patmore, in one of his poems, sums it up thus: 'Love transfigures life, and religion transfigures love.' Good works are often of the I-I variety; love becomes I-Thou. God's work is done through the whole of creation, through those who do not necessary recognize him, and such love of which Paul speaks and Shakespeare celebrates is one derived from outside of ourselves; indeed, it is one that may well surprise us that we are capable of it.

Social science reveals facts which religion speaks of intuitively. Eric Fromm in *The Art of Loving* says that part of man's uniqueness is of his self-awareness and the awareness of his world.[16] The love or attachment of animals, he says, is of an instinctive kind, but when man lacks love, when he experiences separateness, anxiety is aroused in him. Fromm goes so far as to say that 'it is, indeed, the source of all anxiety.' The story of Adam and Eve he interprets by saying that 'after man and woman have become aware of themselves and of each other, they are aware of their own separateness, and of their differences, inasmuch as they belong to different sexes. But while recognising their separateness they remain strangers, because they have not learned to love each other (as is also made clear by the fact that Adam defends himself by blaming Eve, rather than trying to defend her). *The awareness of human separation, without reunion by love, is the source of shame. It is at the same time the source of guilt and anxiety'* (Fromm's italics).

The work of social scientists, and John Bowlby in particular, has shown us the damaging effects of lovelessness and separation but they only confirm the insight of religion.

It is useful at this stage to refer a little more to different kinds of love. According to C. S. Lewis, love is of four kinds.[17] These are *eros*, the love of man for woman, sexual love; *phileo*, the love of man for man, humanitarian love; *agape*, the love between friends; and *caritas*, divine love. God is present wherever love, of whatever kind, is manifested ('All love is of God', as John says.)

Freud and Jung have spoken of love and offered important insights into our own feelings and motivations, our 'irrational' behaviour, which have deepened our understanding of ourselves and extended our sense of our own humanity. But neither Freud nor Jung speak of love as referred to here. Their philosophies do not envisage the self-giving love, the life-transforming force which Paul speaks of. While the Christian acknowledges the truth of some of their insights and their worth, he cannot regard them as a total explanation, nor see Freudian or Jungian concepts of love as substitutes for Christian love.

CHRISTIANS AND SOCIETY

At the most basic level social work is engaged in the relief of suffering, whether the social worker is inclined to see that as best achieved, on the one hand, by individual casework, or, on the other, by political, community-based action, with all the varieties of social work intervention in between. The perspective of the Christian social worker is not confined by the limits of a particular situation but his perspective goes beyond space and time. He conceives of what he does and what he observes and experiences in the context of what has been called 'man in cosmos' rather than 'man in the world'. Thus, the sacramental and social concern are linked in an eschatological tension.

Yet, at times, the church acts as if humanist social concern called the tune; so that statements and actions are made to seem rooted not in the eternal, but in the secular, and as good in themselves. This has been at the expense of developing a theology of social concern; a disregard of the sacramental perspectives; and a failure to enquire where the understandings of the world and faith converge and depart. It is this which spills over into the particular case of social work and Christian understandings.

Christianity from its earliest beginnings has been marked by an ambivalence about the status it accorded to the world. The early Christians, expecting the second coming at any minute, may have tended to play down a concern about the world they expected so soon to be transformed by God's action rather than their own. Augustine, in the fifth century, reflects this in his view of the two cities – the City of Jerusalem, perfect, not through any making by man, through the providence of God; and the City of Babylon, where all is corruption and simple human endeavour is doomed to disappointment even before it begins. But the idea of the two cities can also be taken to symbolize the Christian life in the world, being *in* it but not *of* it. So the Christian derives his values from elsewhere, though he works in the world, and he can only work effectively in the world and appreciate his own life and endeavours, their limitations and their place, if his sight is at the same time on the Heavenly City.

The inability to work out a theology of social concern stems from the church's own division between the sacred and the secular. Too often spirituality and transcendence have been seen as a concern for something over and above the world that must needs be considered as separate from the world, as if spirit and matter had no connection. This is a distortion of Christianity. As Richard

O'Brien writes, spirituality is 'the cultivation of a style of life consistent with the presence of the Spirit of the Risen Christ within us and with our status as members of the Body of Christ.'[18] He outlines the four elements of spirituality as 'visionary' (interpreting reality in spiritual terms); 'sacramental' (seeing God in all things); 'relational' (open to the presence and the call of God in other people); and 'transformational' (always in touch with and open to the Spirit of reconciliation, renewal and healing). Thus, while the spiritual has, often at a cost of secular endeavour, been seen at times as being in opposition to the world, it is, in fact, a way of describing looking *at* the world and responding *to* it.

In pre-scientific times all was regarded as numinous. With the coming of science and the initial failure of the church to come to terms with it, spirit was set against matter and dualism created. The duty of Christian theology is to incorporate the findings of science and social science – whether Marxism or Freudianism – in its own understandings where possible rather than seeing them as opposed *by nature*.

THE PERSONAL AND THE POLITICAL

There will, of course, remain differences which are irreconcilable. For example, while Marxism contains insights that enable us to understand the workings of society in certain ways, its view of human nature and its materialism is at odds with Christianity.

Again in Marxism, and in other world-views expressed in social work, a greater emphasis will be placed on the results expected of material and structural change and the efficacy of legislation than in Christianity. Christian social workers will, rightly, support demands for legislation and structural change, being convinced that there are sinful structures just as there are sinful individuals, but systems of society will not of themselves change men for the better. Where they are oppressive or unjust they need changing, and an attempt must be made to allow stunted talents and the good in man to flourish. But this is to allow opportunities; a new man does not come into being, as Marxism believes, through a change in economic circumstances. Original sin, however understood, asserts a flawedness in man, an inability to reach his true potential. Christianity teaches, too, that unless man works with God in the world, then his efforts will be foredoomed to failure, however well-intended.

On this basis the Christian seeks to promote social change while at the same time being aware of his own shortcomings, with a ready awareness that change must come from within and move outward, rather than be imposed. The Old Testament prophet Isaiah seeks a personal response when he says: 'The kind of fasting I want is this: remove the chains of oppression and the yolk of injustice, and let the oppressed go free. Share your food with the hungry and your homes with the homeless poor.' One cannot love the human race and seek to free it from oppression, if one cannot love individuals and live that liberation in one's own life. This is important to remember if collective action is not to founder. Pope Paul VI observed in his 1971 'Call to Action' that 'Legislation is necessary but is not sufficent for setting up true relationships of justice and equality... If beyond legal rules there is no deeper feeling of respect for a service to others then equality before the law can serve as an alibi for flagrant discrimination, continued exploitation and actual contempt.' This parallels Kay McDougall's counsel [19] that social work needs to be a distinctive way of life that would be judged 'by how we are seen to behave towards our clients and towards each other'.

But not only must a change in personal attitudes and personal respect be at the heart of all social change but there must also be a repentance, a virtue that makes the social worker intensely conscious of his own – and his fellows' inability to realize the end which they desire. This is what is meant by original sin. Wrong-doing is something which we all understand, but sin means more than this. It is, as the New Testament word *harmartia* implies, 'to miss the mark'. The 'mark' is perfection: all that we could be as human beings. Sin means acting against what we truly ought to be, and original sin is our fallenness, missing the mark by reason of our imperfect disobedient humanity.

The ability to recognize both collective and individual sinfulness is, Michel Quoist says, 'a proof of maturity.'[20] 'It is often said', he writes 'that men today, and particularly the young are no longer aware of a sense of sin, but that they are more intensely conscious than ever of their responsibility for the collective sin which affects humanity. This attitude, so long as it does not exclude the recognition of personal faults, is a proof of maturity.' Most of us know the difficulty of trying to put into words, to tabulate, our individual shortcomings, yet that does not make us free from sin. At the same time we are usually intensely conscious that somehow we are out of step with what we know we should be, failing to live up to a higher standard, when we all too easily slip back.

The acceptance of personal and worldly imperfection and the faith to struggle against them (with the significance of the struggle itself recognized) are at the centre of the Christian journey and must be a part of a realistic seeking of the social gospel. The Christian may often not be optimistic but he is always hopeful.

HUMILITY AS A SOCIAL WORK VIRTUE

Acceptance of self-fault is a manifestation of humility, a virtue which Lord Longford takes to be characteristically Christian.[21] However, this is a doubtful claim, for it is, for example, an essential element in Buddhism.[22]

Humility is the most elusive of virtues. To admit that one possesses it shows that one doesn't, as in the story of the renowned Bishop Ullathorne who was lecturing on the subject. 'Your Grace,' enquired a student, 'what is the best book on humility?' 'There is only one,' came the reply, 'I wrote it myself.'

In all the literature of social work, in all the discussion of its values, one rarely hears any reference to humility as a prerequisite of good social work practice. And yet religious writers have spoken of it not just in the same breath as love, but arguing that without humility there can be no love. In his letter to the Ephesians, Paul says: 'I beseech you that you walk worthy of the vocation in which you are called with all humility and mildness, with patience, supporting one another in charity, careful to keep the unity of spirit in the bond of peace.' Thomas à Kempis says: 'If we want charity we must make humility our chief aim,' while Theresa of Avila wrote: 'I cannot understand how there is or can be humility without love, or love without humility.' To be humble is not to hold a low opinion of oneself; rather it is to practise self-forgetfulness. In C. S. Lewis' *The Screwtape Letters* when Screwtape advises his nephew Wormwood on the apprentice arts of deceiving human beings about the true nature of goodness. He advises him that God 'would rather that a man thought himself a great architect or a great poet and forget all about it, than that he should spend much time and pains trying to think himself a bad one ...'[23]

Humility needs, therefore, to be a component of compassion; and the latter is not synonomous with pity for pity may assume a superiority of helper to helped. Compassion of the truest kind recognizes in our own condition a potential victim in the position of others – our death, our sadness, our handicap, our old age, our loneliness, our isolation, our wrong-doing.

Social workers who are *conscious* that they *may* be indulging in power or manipulation of clients in their work have within them the seeds of humility. Brandon puts this well when he says: 'Helping ourselves and others is complicated by the situation and the voracious appetite of the ego. It will feed off anything and everything. It (or rather "I") comes between the experiencing of life and the real desire to be liberated and enlightened. Even the most seemingly pure of thoughts and deeds can be subtly transmuted into self-righteousness. Doing good to others can make me even more conscious of the separation between myself and others. "I" can become proud of my own acquisition of personal virtue and feel superior to others.'

Humility, then, demands that the social worker learns from the client and receives in his turn. Christianity has often stressed a necessary detachment from material possessions, and while it also stresses the loss of self, we also find in Buddhism mention of the 'inner acquisitions' in the phrase of Irmgard Schloegl.[24] These she terms as 'notions and views and convictions rather than goods and chattels'. Here there are obvious links with Christian concepts of humility and social work principles like acceptance and non-judgemental attitudes. If the client is truly to be seen as 'a fellow citizen', then he can only ever become so with the full exercise of humility, the lack of professional self-regard and of notions of doing *to*, rather than doing *with*.

PERSONAL RESPONSIBILITY

Any attempt to describe at what point an individual becomes personally responsible for his actions is fraught with difficulties. The belief that human beings are personally responsible for their actions is not a distinguishing feature of Christianity as such: it is one recognized in most faiths and by many who have no religious belief. But a belief in non-judgemental attitudes and a training in psychology and sociology, with their emphasis on the effects of experiences and invironment on human actions, may make social workers at the very least suspicious of a concept of personal responsibility, and at most lead to a disavowal of its validity.

The law, of course, makes very real distinctions when it allows of the idea of diminished responsibility, but this is a regard for a supposedly definable (if not uncontroversial) mental incapacity. The permeation in our culture of psychological wisdom has made the concept of 'sickness' a strong one and many people believe that personal circumstances can explain away certain behaviour.

It can be said, of course, that such considerations are often not the social worker's concern because he does not administer punishment. But he ought to be concerned because the 'treatment' which some forms of social work are said to offer imply a 'sickness'. It is also relevant to the social worker because to work with someone he needs a clear-eyed view of how he regards that person's behaviour. Further, it is relevant because much social work practice is founded upon theories of human behaviour and motivation.

Personal autonomy, whatever reservations we accept about it, is an essential notion if people are to be regarded as moral agents. They have free will; it is what sets them above the animals. People have a destiny which they make (or fail to make) by their own efforts and choices. God does not force obedience for it must be willingly given. In being able to make a choice for good we know that evil exists. In Genesis, mankind chooses evil, men and women choose separation from God, asserting themselves and not God as the centre of the creation, and placing their own interests first.

A person without free will is not a person in a complete and most human sense. He or she is merely a creature of circumstance. While each person is created by God and is of infinite value to him, his or her individuality is marked, in part, by the personal choices which they make. This ability to choose and a recognition of the essential nature of human imperfection (rather than the sum of individual people's imperfections) brings the individual into community with others, stressing his or her common humanity. Thus, the social worker cannot be superior to the client and recognises that 'there, but for the grace of God, go I.' But to seek to explain away or excuse the actions of another is to diminish the person, to make him less than human.

Questions of free will, choice, irrational behaviour and circumstances have become inextricably mixed up with notions of non-judgementalism, and this has been misunderstood. Certainly, social workers should not be concerned with responsibility when that is taken to mean blameworthiness, and the confusion between non-judgementalism and blameworthiness works to the disadvantage of good and effective practice. Butrym discusses her, admittedly tentative, findings after visiting six social services departments.[25] She found that while relationships with clients were in most cases 'benevolent' and that the majority of social workers whom she saw in action and spoke to 'had a genuine commitment to being helpful to their clients', there was frequently a discrepancy between commitment in principle and its actual translation into effective practice. She writes: 'One common manifestation of this was a marked reluctance to make full and explicit assessment of clients' problems before embarking on an action. This seemed partly due to a confusion between professional assessment of a problem and a judgemental view toward the person having the problem.'

The true understanding of non-judgementalism finds a parallel in the Christian belief in God's acceptance of us all – with all our faults and through no merit on our part. Paul Tillich in *The Shaking of the Foundations* writes: '*You are accepted*, accepted by that which is greater than you, and the name of which you do not know. Do not ask for the name now; perhaps you will find it later. Do not try to do anything; do not try to perform anything; do not intend anything. *Simply accept that you are!...* After such an experience we may not be better than before, and we may not believe more than before. But everything is transformed. In that moment of grace, grace conquers sin, and reconciliation bridges the gulf of estrangement.'[26]

Tillich is describing religious experience and God's acceptance of us as we are, as we turn to him. And while the relationship of the social worker and the client is one between two sinful individuals, nevertheless the social worker's non-judgementalism, his acceptance of the client, implies no approval of behaviour, nor any denial of his own personal values. It is to do with the necessary separation of judgement about values from feelings towards people. It may be called, perhaps more helpfully and accurately, non-condemnatory, the ability to accept others as they are; in the old religious phrase 'to hate the sin and love the sinner.' If the social worker is non-judgemental in this way; if he can make these distinctions and this separation; if he is truly accepting of another; then he is exhibiting a profound humility because he recognizes his own potential difficulties and failings (indeed, perhaps his *actual* difficulties and failings) in another.

SUFFERING

Facing the fact of suffering is one of the most distressing, perplexing and difficult of our tasks as human beings. Illness, misfortune and death are visited upon the just and the unjust and the questions Job asked are those of every person.

The problem of suffering has been a critical one in religious writing. It has often been posed in misleading terms as a choice between God and suffering, as if the existence of one cancelled out the other. Christianity has taken the fact of suffering to its very heart. Its most potent symbol is the broken, dying, isolated figure of a man on a cross. But the cross is but a prelude – failure precedes triumph, life comes out of death, Good Friday's emptiness and gloom come before the flowering garden and the empty tomb of Easter Day. The cross is about the ultimate goodness of divine purposes, but to believe this is not a once-and-for-all thing, a spiritual bolt-hole against the harsh realities of the world, for the redemption continues to be worked out in ourselves and through ourselves.

Through the incarnation – the Word made flesh – Christ became like one of us and so suffered with us. The Christian God is, then, not a remote, unfeeling figure, but one who has been man, who can suffer for us and with us, as a human parent can for a child. As the Psalmist said, 'If I go down to Hell, thou art there also.'

Social workers work with suffering – increasing incapacity, loss, death, awful misfortune. But to say that suffering is inevitable and unavoidable in our world is not to be complacent about it or to counsel stoicism in the face of it. Our natural response is anger, bitterness, resentment, doubt. But that cannot be the end of it. If it were, suffering would destroy us. We have to take suffering and make what we can of it. How each person reacts is unpredictable. Mary Craig looks to a healthy and positive attitude when she writes: 'The value of suffering does not lie in the pain of it. Two people can go through the same painful experience, one can be destroyed by it, the other achieve an extra dimension. The real tragedy of suffering is the wasted opportunity.'[27] This is not pious or wishful thinking. Mary Craig's own experience, with two severely mentally handicapped sons, an experience replicated many times over, in other ways, by other parents, is testimony enough.

In other circumstances, suffering has its lessons. Pain and suffering can lay bare the essential self, help us to learn what is truly important, strip us of everything extraneous to our true natures. Pierre d'Harcourt, relating his experiences as a prisoner in the Buchenwald concentration camp, explains the point:

'All I know is that when it became hardest of all for men to behave like human beings they spread their wings and rose to great heights; and when the strains and temptations were removed they sank into the mud.

'In their heart of hearts they may have felt, as I did, that, in its way, it was the life of the camp that was the true life, the life that bore witness to what really counted in humanity, the Spirit...

'This for me is the first lesson of the camp – that it made beasts of some men and saints of others. And the second lesson is that it is hard to predict who will be the saint and who the beast when the time of trial comes. Only one thing prevailed – strength of character. Cleverness, creativeness, learning, all went down; only real goodness survived.'[28]

At times, those who work with suffering people can too easily see the failure to 'cure' or to overcome affliction as a professional failure and a human tragedy. But to believe otherwise does not mean that professional integrity is sacrificed to personal conviction or, in the case of the Christian social worker, that beliefs about the place of suffering are imposed on the suffering client. (Though, conversely, at times a client who does share Christian convictions may welcome discussion – not with a 'professional' social worker but with a social worker who sheds his professional mien to offer his own thoughts – but this can only be at the client's own request and questioning.) Viewed in a finite perspective, death, for example, may be seen as a disaster, as a failure, as an end, and a rather pointless one at that. The hospice movement, however, has now begun to teach us that the care of the dying, the assistance to a peaceful death, is itself a calling for social work, medical and nursing staff.

To heal is not necessarily to make better – wholeness of person is about maturity, acceptance (which is not resignation), about counting the quality and not the quantity of life. If this healing produces physical well-being, as it may, then that is a bonus.

The need then is to hold, in what at times is a difficult balance, a recognition of the limits of human intervention, an acceptance of suffering and the desire to do all we can to overcome it. Those who believe in a finite existence may find this the more difficult to accept than those whose vision is transcendental, but, as Zofia Butrym points out, to accept this tension and hold the equilibrium is essential in truly professional social work. She says that an essential element of what is called 'ego strength', which is itself required by the effective and mature social worker, is 'a capacity to accept the place of suffering in human life as inevitable and even natural and to couple that acceptance with a firm commitment to prevent and alleviate that suffering which is open to human intervention. In contrast, I would see a total rejection of suffering and an unwarranted complacency toward it as inimical to good social work.'[29]

Each person suffers in his own way, some with and for others, some alone. Social workers are called upon to try to help all of them, remembering their own suffering. To ask why there should be pain and suffering is to pose an unanswerable question; easier to ask: 'Why not?' To hold the balance between acceptance of suffering and a wish to do something to overcome it, as Butrym counsels, is the most practical response and is to say, in another way: 'Take up your cross and follow me.' Such is not only part of a theology of social work but of living.

CHRISTIAN SOCIAL WORK IN ACTION

The Christian does not bring to life's situations a set of propositions to which he gives intellectual assent. He does not live on the basis of credal statements. 'Theology is not to be learned, but to be lived; it is not to be thought, but to be experienced,' as C.S. Song says.[30] He goes on to say that 'the doing of theology takes place where a difficult decision has to be taken, be it personal or social. It is done where a value judgement has to be made, where choice between good and evil cannot be avoided.' John Vincent makes the same points when he defines 'political theology' as 'doing theology in the context of politics.'[31]

We can now see that there are important meeting-points and divergences between Christian and social work understandings. Their practical working out, the resolution of conflicts, must come from a 'social work theology', which, to paraphrase Vincent's words, means to do theology in the context of social work. Such a theology attempts to discover the practical meaning of Christianity in social work. No area of social work is invulnerable to this test – social work in hospices as much as social workers urging pressures for change for greater equality and justice; social work in child care to send children into the world, as much as social work with elderly people at the end of their lives when they are, so to speak, gathered in.

In this the social worker shares an obligation with all people, as workers, as parents, as children, as neighbours, as citizens. The end result is not the revelation of certainty, for the only certainty is beyond space and time. It is the life lived in struggle, on the pilgrim's path, to try to learn, whatever the particular calling, what it means to be fully human.

Notes

1   L. E. Elliott Binns, *English Thought 1806-1900 – The Theological Aspect*, Longman, 1956.
2   Kay McDougall, 'Obligations of a Profession', *Social Work Today*, September 1970.
3   Martin Davies, *The Essential Social Worker*, Heinemann Educational/ Community Care, 1981 (second edition 1985), p.9.
4   Martin Davies, *The Essential Social Worker*, p.4.
5   Barclay Report, *Social Workers: Their Roles and Tasks*, National Institute for Social Work, Bedford Square Press, 1982.

6 Quoted in 'Ethics and the Social Worker', Florence Emmett, *Social Work and Social Values*, Volume III (Ed. Eileen Younghusband), Allen and Unwin, 1967.

7 Barbara Wootton, *Social Science and Social Pathology*, Allen and Unwin, 1959.

8 Smith and van Krieken, *British Journal of Social Work*, February 1984.

9 Noel Timms, *Social Work Values: An Enquiry*, Routledge and Kegan Paul, 1983.

10 Felix Biestek, *The Casework Relationship*, Allen and Unwin 1961.

11 Zofia Butrym, *The Nature of Social Work*, MacMillan, 1976.

12 Quoted in H. Prins, 'Motivation in Social Work', *Social Work Today*, 18 April, 1974.

13 Raymond Plant, *Social and Moral Theory in Casework*, Routledge and Kegan Paul, 1970.

14 J. B. Phillips, *Making Men Whole*, Fontana, 1952.

15 Jerusalem Bible.

16 Eric Fromm, *The Art of Loving*, Allen and Unwin, 1957.

17 C. S. Lewis, *The Four Loves*, Fontana, 1963.

18 Richard O'Brien, *Catholicism*, Geoffrey Chapman, 1984.

19 See note 2 above.

20 Michel Quoist, *Christ is Alive!*, Gill/MacMillan, 1971.

21 Lord Longford, *Humility*, Fontana, 1969.

22 See David Brandon, *Zen in the Art of Helping*, Routledge and Kegan Paul, 1976.

23 C. S. Lewis, *The Screwtape Letters*, Geoffrey Bles, 1942.

24 Irmgard Schloegl, *The Wisdom of the Zen Masters*, Sheldon Press, 1975.

25 'Ethical and Value Systems that Characterise Social Work Education' in Louise S. Bandler (Editor), *Education for Clinical Social Work Practice: Continuity and Change*, Pergamon Press, 1983.

26 Paul Tillich, *The Shaking of the Foundations*, SCM 1949.

27 Mary Craig, *Blessings*, Hodder and Stoughton, 1979.

28 Pierre d'Harcourt, *The Real Enemy*, Longman, 1967.

29 From *Education for Clinical Social Work Practice* – see note 24 above.

30 C.S. Song, *Third Eye Theology*, Lutterworth Press, 1981.

31 John Vincent, 'Doing Theology', *Agenda for Prophets*, ed. D. Haslam and R. Ambler, Bowerdean Press, 1980.

Contributors

Terry Drummond, born in Yorkshire, is a Captain in the Church Army, for which organization he is planning officer, having formerly held responsibility for field social work in England and Wales. A Church Army officer for 13 years, he has done community work in Leicester and for four years worked with single homeless people and alcoholics in London. He is a joint founder of Christians in Social Work. Publications include *Alcoholism* (Mowbrays, 1981) and (with Mary Pepper) *Liberation Theology and British Christians* (Jubilee Publications, 1984), also *Poverty and Theology, Towards a Renewed Understanding* and *Essays Catholic and Radical* (Bowerden Press, 1983). He edited *Catholicism and Conflict* (Jubilee Publications, 1982) and (with Kenneth Leech) *Letters from Seven Churches* (Jubilee Publications, 1984).

Peter Gilbert, a Jerseyman, was educated at the Benedictine Abbey of Worth and after five years in the army, took a degree in modern history at Balliol College, Oxford. After qualifying at Sussex University he worked for some years as a generic social worker before taking up his present post as team leader at the Forest Hospital (mental handicap), Horsham, in 1981. He is the co-author of two information handbooks for parents of mentally handicapped children and contributed the chapter on the role of the social worker to the 1985 successor to 'Tredgold's', *Mental Handicap: a Multi-Disciplinary Approach*. He is chairman of the Bishop of Arundel and Brighton's working party on mental handicap and a member of the specialist panel for the English National Board's post-qualifying course for nurses in the field of mental handicap. He was the social work contributor for the recent ENB training pack for Registered Mental Handicap Nurses, *Caring for People with Mental Handicap*. He is also author of *Mental Handicap: A Practical Guide for Social Workers* (1985).

John Gladwin was ordained in the Church of England and taught at St John's College, Durham. He was director of the Shaftesbury Project on Christian Involvement in Society before taking up his present post as secretary of the General Synod Board for Social Responsibility of the Church of England. He has written and contributed to a number of books concerning Christian thinking about ethical, political and social issues. He is author of *God's People in God's World* (IVP, 1978) and edited *Dropping the Bomb* (Hodder and Stoughton, 1984).

Lydia Gladwin is Director of Social Work for the Church of England's London Diocesan Board for Social Responsibility. She is a past chairman of the Social Workers' Christian Fellowship and has written articles for Christian publications and a research project on long-term substitute care for children. She spent fifteen years in local authority social services.

Chris Hanvey qualified at Barnett House, Oxford, and worked in social work in Edinburgh. He has been a field worker in Yorkshire and a residential worker in Warwickshire, after which he became a district manager with Coventry Social Services Department. He is presently principal assistant in the department. He is an editorial adviser to *Community Care* and a frequent contributor to social work journals, as well as being an assessor for the *British Journal of Social Work*. He is the author of *Social Work with Mentally Handicapped People* (Heinemann Educational, 1981).

Andrew Henderson was ordained in the Church of England in 1962 and qualified as a psychiatric social worker in 1965. Apart from an excursion into education for two years, he has worked in four London social services departments and is currently director of social services for the Royal Borough of Kensington and Chelsea. He has been a member of the Southwark Diocesan Priest Worker Chapter since it began and contributed a chapter to *Stewards of the Mysteries of God* (Darton, Longman & Todd, 1979).

Bob Holman started his career in social work as a child care officer and subsequently moved into academic life with appointments at Birmingham and Glasgow Universities before becoming professor of social administration at the University of Bath. Since 1976, he has worked for the Roundhill (formerly Southdown) Community Project which is part of the Children's Society. He is a frequent contributor to the social work press and his main books are *Poverty: Explanations of Social Deprivation* (Martin Robertson, 1978) and *Kids at the Door* (Blackwell, 1981). He has also written, under a pseudonym, *More than a Friend* (Lion Publishing, 1984).

David Lane was born in Derbyshire, read classics and moral sciences at Cambridge University and qualified in residential work at Newcastle University. From 1964 he worked for six years at Aycliffe School, first as a teacher/housemaster and then as senior housemaster. With his wife, Kathleen, he jointly ran an assessment centre in Somerset. In 1972, he became a social work education adviser with the Central Council for Education and Training in Social Work. From 1975 he was assistant director (day and residential care), Hillingdon social services department. In 1985 he was appointed Director of Social Services, Wakefield Council. He is a member of CCETSW, a governor of the National Institute for Social Work and a past president of the Social Care Association. His publications include *Why Care?* (edited with Keith White) (SCA) and *Stress* (SCA). He was compiler of the SCA's *Bonnington Report* and was co-editor of *The Quiet Evolution* (MacMillan).

Brian Munday is senior lecturer in social work at the University of Kent, Canterbury, where he has worked since 1971. He previously worked as a probation officer and a psychiatric social worker and taught mature students at the North London Polytechnic. He is actively involved with voluntary organisations and volunteers and is joint editor of *Volunteers in the Personal Social Services* (Tavistock Press, 1984). He has written articles and addressed conferences on various aspects of Christianity and social work.

Katherine Mundy was born in London and trained at Croydon College. She worked for ten years in local authority social work, predominantly in inner city areas. Formerly a social worker for Church Housing Association, she is now training officer for Job Concern (Mitcham), an unemployment project. She is a past NALGO shop steward and a joint founder of Christians in Social Work.

W. J. Patterson graduated from the New University of Ulster in 1971 in social administration and then spent a year living and working in Brussels, where he also took a diploma in sociology at the Free University. He returned to the NUU to complete his studies and gain a professional qualification in social work. Since 1973 he has been employed in various posts by the Northern Health and Social Services Board and is currently assistant principal social worker with responsibility for the family and child care programme of the district of Coleraine, Ballymoney and Moyle. He is a founder member and trustee of the Irish Christian Study Centre. He is the author of *Social Work's Theory of Man* (NUU, 1975).

Terry Philpot, born in London, has been editor of *Community Care* since 1978, having been previously deputy editor of *Nursing Mirror*. Prior to that he held various posts with magazines and newspapers. He has worked as a literacy tutor and been involved in a variety of community organizations, as well as serving as an elected member of a local authority. He has edited three other books. He is a magistrate and founder-chairman and a trustee of the Third World Group, a charity.

Julia Staples was trained as a nurse at the United Sheffield Hospitals. She then spent ten years as a residential social worker, employed by Sheffield Family and Community Services Department, where she worked mainly in establishments caring for children, and for a short time she worked with elderly people. During this period she completed the Certificate in the Residential Care of Children and Young People course at the North London Polytechnic and the senior course at Bristol University. From 1980 she worked as officer-in-charge of Spire Lodge short-term care centre for mentally handicapped children and their families, a Derbyshire County Council resource in Chesterfield. In 1985 she was appointed administrator of the West of England Friends Housing Society. She has written for the social work press.

Keith White is assistant director of Mill Grove, East London, which was founded by his grandfather. Keith White was born there and has been based there since 1975. After gaining a degree in English at Oxford, he engaged in research at Edinburgh University, and also worked as a community worker and social worker in Scotland. He was a member of the Barclay committee and is a member of the general purposes committee of the National Council of Voluntary Child Care Organisations. He is vice-chairman of the Mayflower Family Centre, East London and president of the Social Care Association 1984/5. He was a lay minister of a non-conformist church for four years and is a lecturer in sociology at Spurgeons's Theological College. He is a frequent contributor to the social work press and is an editorial advisor to *Community Care*. His publications include *A Place for Us*, *In His Image*, *Caring for Children* (with Chris Payne), *Why Care?* (with David Lane), and *The Best of In Residence*, volumes 1 and 2 (with Chris Payne).